THE CARDINAL

Thomas Joseph Winning
1925–2001

In recalling Cardinal Winning's generous and committed service as priest and bishop, I join in giving thanks to God for the many blessings bestowed upon the Church through his ministry. During those long years, this zealous pastor encouraged the communities he served in faith and Christian living, and was particularly outstanding in defence of life and commitment to the poor.

I am confident that his example will inspire all the members of the Church in Scotland to grow in their love of Christ and to increase their resolve to serve their brothers and sisters in a spirit of Christian charity.

Joannes Paulus II

THE CARDINAL

THOMAS JOSEPH WINNING

1925–2001

EDITED BY RONNIE CONVERY

BIOGRAPHY BY BRIAN MCGEACHAN

PHOTOGRAPHY BY PAUL MCSHERRY

OFFICIAL TRIBUTE

First published in 2001 by
Lindsay Publications,
Glasgow.

ISBN 1 898169 27 6

A CIP record of this publication is available from the British Library.

Designed and typeset by Eric Mitchell, Glasgow and
C & R Graphics, Cumbernauld.

Printed and bound in Scotland by J. Thomson Colour Printers Limited Glasgow.

WHEN I RECEIVED THE NEWS that I was to be elevated to the College of Cardinals, one of the first phone calls I received was from Tom Winning. He was genuinely delighted at the news, and he spoke eagerly of all we could do together as brother Cardinals from these islands for the Church.

Alas, out time together as Cardinals was short. Just four months. I was stunned by the news on that fateful Sunday of June 17 2001 that Cardinal Tom had died. I had spoken to him just a few days earlier and he seemed so well and so cheerful.

His loss is still being felt, not only in Scotland, but across the UK and beyond. In my travels I meet people who recall his kindness, his courage and his unfailing good humour.

It is that good humour which I shall recall most easily. No conversation with Cardinal Tom ended without a smile or a hearty laugh. He had the gift of putting everyone at ease in his presence, from pauper to prince.

I am delighted that the decision has been taken to produce this official tribute book in memory of the man whose work, commitment and bravery shaped modern Scottish Catholicism.

Many of the tributes paid to Cardinal Tom by the great and good are included in this volume, but I am particularly glad to see tributes, too, from people who are not public figures, but who knew the Cardinal and felt his loss deeply.

Cardinal Tom was intensely proud of "his ain folk", and never happier than when swamped in a crowd of Glaswegians, joking and clasping hands, recognising faces and encouraging people to live out their faith.

His episcopal motto was "Caritas Christi Urget Nos" – we are spurred on by the love of Christ. His ministry as priest, bishop and cardinal was all about putting that motto into practice . . . the love of Jesus Christ spurred him on to encourage, support and help others to deepen and share their faith.

My hope is that this little book will continue that work.

May all who come across this volume in the months and years to come, be inspired just a little, to persevere, to keep the faith, and to aim for that final prize of heaven which we trust our dear Cardinal Tom is now enjoying in its fullness.

With every blessing

+Cormac Murphy. O'Connor

+Cormac Cardinal Murphy O'Connor
Archbishop of Westminster,
President of the Bishops' Conference of England and Wales.

I FIRST GOT TO KNOW the late Cardinal when, as a young priest, I was on retreat at Nunraw Abbey. The Cardinal was then Archbishop of Glasgow and I wondered just how I would approach him and how he would treat me! Basically, as so many people have found, no barriers existed – and he made sure that we had adequate time off from our retreat at Nunraw to visit Dunbar, enjoy ice-cream there and also visit the toy shops!

The memory of that occasion came back to me on my visits to Rome – with myself, as Archbishop and Archbishop Winning, a Cardinal. Despite frequent meetings which we attended at two successive Synods of Bishops, the Cardinal always found that 'escape' when he could really be himself. On these occasions, it was invariably to the Borgo Pio, a small street near St Peter's where there was an excellent plate of spaghetti on offer and again that tour of the toy shops!

The Cardinal has often been described as having the 'common touch', and an ability to relate to anyone. This indeed helped him in his role as leader of the Catholic Church in Scotland, while also being one of the closest advisers of Pope John Paul II, as a Cardinal of the Church.

When thinking of his achievements, one must never forget that he had a razor-sharp intellect; and that fearlessness, which enabled him to speak out in defence of the teachings of the Church, welcome or unwelcome.

Having been President of the Bishops' Conference of Scotland since the death of Cardinal Gray, he knew the members of our Conference intimately. He was to us both a leader and a friend. While we were together at our residential conferences and our in-service courses, he could always break any tensions by his ready jokes – while always ensuring that business in hand was attended to and clear leadership given to the whole Church in Scotland, as indeed often to the whole Christian community.

His death has been a tremendous loss to us all. However, I am sure that this book will be a happy reminder of the man we knew and loved and who inspired the Catholic Church in Scotland and throughout the world in innumerable ways.

+ *Keith Patrick*

+Keith Patrick O'Brien
Archbishop of St Andrews and Edinburgh

ACKNOWLEDGEMENTS

I WISH TO ACKNOWLEDGE the assistance I have had in bringing this official tribute to Cardinal Thomas Winning to fruition. Firstly my thanks to Harry Conroy, editor of the *Scottish Catholic Observer* who originally suggested a book of this kind. My thanks also go to Ignatius Kusiak, managing director of the *Catholic Herald Limited*, owners of the *Scottish Catholic Observer*, Mgr Peter Smith, Chancellor of the Archdiocese of Glasgow and Donald MacDonald, proprietor of Lindsay Publications who agreed at a very early stage to support this venture.

Thanks also go to Paul McSherry who provided the majority of the photographs contained in this book and for his help in selection, Brian McGeachan who wrote the biographical material and Ian MacNicol who provided research assistance.

Much effort was required to publish this volume so soon after the death of the Cardinal. I should like to thank in a special way our Production Consultant, Eric Mitchell, who made sure that we did not allow deadlines to slip and also Robert Miller, proprietor of C&R Graphics whose staff produced such a high quality publication.

My greatest debt of gratitude goes to the late Cardinal Winning's family who provided wonderful archive material of his early life and the later times he so treasured with them – far from the glare of publicity.

Within the pages of this book we have published a few of the thousands of tributes recorded in the press or sent directly to the Archdiocese of Glasgow following the death of the Cardinal. I would like to thank all who took the time to send their tributes and memories of Cardinal Winning. These are a great comfort to his family.

Of all the tributes which arrived, I would like to signal one in particular which summed up his impact on so many people. It was written on the back of a postcard bought in Lisbon in 1967 (when the Cardinal's beloved Celtic won the *European Cup*) which had been carefully treasured for 34 years. The card was unsigned, and the message was short:

> *"To a friend I never knew, but always knew I had."*

It would be hard to sum up the impact of the life of Thomas Joseph Cardinal Winning on countless thousands of people more appropriately.
Requiescat in pace.

Ronnie Convery
Editor
October 2001

DEDICATION

This book is dedicated to all the babies whose lives have been saved and the mothers whose lives have been transformed by the Pro-Life Initiative founded by Cardinal Thomas Winning.

TRIBUTES

He made a very distinguished contribution to the Catholic Church in Scotland and to Scottish public life over many years and will be sadly missed.

Her Majesty, The Queen

His strong moral leadership and commitment to social justice were renowned.

Rt Hon Tony Blair MP
Prime Minister

Tom Winning was someone who never forgot where he came from. Scotland has lost one of her greatest sons. I will miss him.

Henry McLeish MSP
First Minister of Scotland

He was a great ambassador for the Catholic Church and for Scotland and never tired of fighting against injustice and poverty. He was an inspiration to all and his wisdom will be sorely missed across many sectors of Scottish life.

John Swinney MSP
Leader of the SNP

Cardinal Winning's death will be a great loss, not just to Scotland's Roman Catholic community, but more widely throughout civic Scotland.

Whilst not always agreeing with him, I always treated his views with considerable respect, not least because of the conviction and sincerity with which they were expressed. Scotland is a poorer place without him.

Jim Wallace MSP
Leader of the Scottish Liberal Democrats

He was one of the most eminent and distinguished churchmen Scotland has ever produced. He was a great moral leader and a staunch advocate of the values and principles which should underpin our society.

David McLetchie MSP
Leader of the Scottish Conservative Party

I had the privilege of meeting him on a number of occasions and was struck by the warmth of his personality and the strength of his moral convictions. He was a man whose reputation was almost as great in Ireland as in his native land. His untimely passing is deeply felt here.

Bertie Ahern
Taoiseach, Dublin, Ireland

People from all walks of life in Glasgow and people of all religions and those of no religion responded to his very welcoming way. My wife and I were fortunate to have been in the company of Cardinal Thomas Winning on many occasions just as the people of Glasgow have been in his company throughout his ministry. We all loved him and will miss him greatly.

Rt Hon Alex Mosson
Lord Provost of Glasgow

+THOMAS JOSEPH CARDINAL WINNING
1925–2001

A LIFE WELL LIVED

IN THE YEAR BEFORE HE DIED, Cardinal Winning was asked if he had ever had any doubts about his faith. "Doubts?" came his bemused reply. "Why ever would I have doubts?"

That rock-like faith which was to serve him so well was imbibed almost with his mother's milk.

His birth to Thomas and Agnes Winning on 3 June 1925 in the working-class area of Craigneuk, Lanarkshire showed little promise of the potential that was to come. It was a grim landscape, literally and metaphorically, and poverty was the norm for the majority of people in the area. Tom's father, like many of his generation, experienced hard times and unemployment.

Initially a coal-miner, Thomas senior enlisted in the Gordon Highlanders seeing action in the trenches of the First World War. Perhaps those experiences of warfare may have proved instrumental in shaping the future Cardinal's views on conflict and the importance of diplomacy as an alternative to acts of aggression. Tom recalled years later: "I remember as a child, caught up as children are in wonderment at apparently exciting times, asking my father what he had done during the war. He brought me down to earth, not by recounting deeds of valour, but by recalling the stench of the mud and the beast-infestation which plagued the men in the trenches."

He added: "He taught me a very valid lesson early on. The lesson that war is never glamorous." As it turned out, neither was peace.

Thomas senior, returning home from the war, found civilian life far from easy. Fed-up at the lack of opportunities afforded to his generation he left for the United States and later worked in various short-term jobs in Canada. His travels in the New World, however, failed to persuade him to settle in these countries. Before long he returned to Craigneuk.

Now in his thirties he struggled to find work in the mines and steel industry, and like many Catholics, was refused job after job because of his religious faith. But his personal life was to change dramatically when he met and married Agnes Canning, the second youngest child of a family of sixteen brothers and sisters.

By marrying into such a large family he acquired a large collection of in-laws and a network of relations, like his own, steeped in Catholicism.

The rituals of Catholic life, the world of novenas and sodalities, of Sacred Heart pictures and Rosary processions was the context into which, one June day in 1925, baby Thomas Joseph was born.

No-one in those far off days could have imagined that one day he would be a Prince of the Church.

The family was completed with the arrival, not long afterwards, of another baby, Margaret, who was later to be a teacher.. They were active parishioners of St Patrick's Church in Shieldmuir and Tom's father was a member of the Saint Vincent de Paul Society, helping those even poorer than himself.

Many years later he recalled in an interview with the writer and broadcaster

Kenneth Roy those early days: "My father was very, very even-tempered. I met a man once who said, 'I worked beside your father when I was sixteen years of age, and he gave me a belling-off for swearing. I've never used a bad word since.' The more mature I got, the more I appreciated the integrity of the man."

It was Tom's mother who was manager of the tiny household budget. "I never knew I was poor. I was as well dressed as anybody in the community. The only thing was, we never got a holiday. I remember the folk next door always went to Portobello for a week. Came back with whelks!

"When I asked my mother whether we could go on holiday too, she said, 'All right, we'll go next year provided you're willing to eat margarine every day instead of butter!' I

Tom with his mother and sister.

told her to forget it."

As Tom and his sister Margaret grew up their home consisted of two rooms and a kitchen, and like many families in the area, their father continued to seek employment with little or no success. Tom's schooling began in St Patrick's Primary, Shieldmuir, and – apart from Maths – he absorbed the lessons easily, showing an aptitude for study and learning which was to be life-long. Teachers and fellow pupils remember him as a hard-working and popular boy who walked every day to school and never skipped lessons.

The daily walks, however, were not without their dangers. Despite his early devotion to his Church he often adopted a pragmatic stance: "There was one part of the main street down to the school where you were apt to be caught by the jersey and asked if you were Catholic or Protestant. Many's

Tom and Margaret.

the time I denied my Faith to get to school on time," he recalled more than half a century later with a twinkle in his eye.

At the age of ten Tom was asked by a curate of St Patrick's, Father James Cuthbert Ward if he would like to join the church choir. He readily agreed to go along and soon became a permanent fixture. A year later he was approached with the invitation to become an altar boy. It seemed then that the boy's life was moving in an inevitable direction.

Trained under the guidance of Father Bartholomew Atkinson he proved adept at picking up the Latin responses and soon grew to love participating in the morning Mass before going to school. The rules for altar duty were fairly strict by today's standards: the priest was apt to check that the altar boys' fingernails were clean before they were due to serve Mass!

At this time Tom made the transition from primary to secondary school, attending Our Lady's High School in Motherwell. The co-ed establishment also produced another bishop (Maurice Taylor of Galloway) and many priests. When asked years later what interested him at school, he replied: "*Saturdays*".

Although a characteristically tongue-in-cheek response, he never claimed to be a dedicated academic. "I wasn't all that enamoured of it. If you were academically good people were interested in you, if you weren't – well, I was probably glad to get shot of it."

As thoughts turned to the future there was one nagging thought in his mind: what about the priesthood? The devotional, sometimes remote, but always respected priests he grew up with became role models. He admired the sacrifices they made for the Church and the parishioners who seemed to depend on them for physical as well as spiritual support and solace.

During his time as an altar boy he adopted a prayer of St Ignatius that summed up his own philosophy:

> *Lord, teach me to be generous, to serve you as you deserve.*
> *To give and not to count the cost,*
> *To fight and not to heed the wounds,*
> *To labour and not to ask for any reward,*
> *Save for the knowing that I do God's Holy Will.*

Interestingly, he revealed many years later, "My second choice would have been a doctor or a lawyer, something with a kick in it: defending people, bringing them back to health."

Despite his closeness to his parents, however, he remained reluctant to share his decision with them. He was embarrassed. "I felt, maybe I wasn't good enough, that I was aspiring to something too big."

At the age of thirteen he spoke to Father Atkinson about his desire to enter the priesthood. The priest encouraged him to continue with his secondary school studies, and then go on to the major seminary. He was warned not to go to Blairs College – the junior seminary – because of its notoriously bad food!

His parents were delighted with the news, and his extended family of aunts, uncles and cousins felt proud of the calling of their young relative.

As an avid reader of the Catholic press from an early age, Tom had followed with interest developments within the Vatican and the Church's position on the growing political problems in Europe. Mussolini in Italy, Franco in Spain and Hitler in Germany, held power. The Spanish Civil War had a particular fascination for him and, as a young boy, he sympathised with Franco's armies, fighting, as he saw it, the beast of Communism.

In 1939 there was a papal election following the death of Pope Pius XI, and the new Pontiff, Eugenio Pacelli took the name Pius XII in honour of his predecessor. Little did Tom know that just a few years later, the ascetic and saintly Pontiff would receive him in audience as a newly ordained priest.

That same year, Thomas senior embarked upon a route out of his enforced idleness when a relative taught him how to make sweets. The future Cardinal enjoyed recalling those days: "He used to buy bags and bags of sugar from the Co-op, and he would go round the shops and offer his sweets for sale. All sorts of tablet and boilings, and they even got to the stage of marzipan walnuts. They were the luxury items."

Tom at a family celebration during his student days.

Mindful of the watchful glare of the means test at the time, Tom's father informed them of his sideline. The rules allowed him to make four shillings profit a week. The parish priest told him to make as much as he could!

Young Tom passed his Highers at the age of seventeen, and after applying to enter the seminary travelled to Glasgow for an initial interview.

His experience of Latin, from his six years as an altar boy, stood him in good stead, as the selection panel of Canons and Monsignori asked him to read a page in the language of Cicero. When asked why he wanted to be a priest, Tom replied, "I want to leave the world a better place than I found it." Later he was to admit that his answer was rather grandiose, but it seemed to do the trick. The panel accepted his application and he was set on the first rung of the ladder to the priesthood.

Facing him was a two-year stint at Blairs College, in Aberdeen, where senior seminarians studied philosophy. Owing to the war all the seminaries in Spain, Rome and Paris were closed. Unfortunately, Tom did not settle comfortably into Blairs College. He felt homesick, and he struggled to adapt to a routine so unlike the home life he had been accustomed to.

In later years he reflected that this may have been because of his instinctive feel for the practical application of Catholicism, rather than the theoretical. Although more than capable of handling the lessons and passing the exams, his longing to be of service to the people in the parishes and at grassroots level was uppermost in his thoughts.

As a result the student priest looked forward to his bursts of freedom, and prayed that the two years would pass quickly.

In 1944 Tom's education continued at St Peter's, the theology seminary in Bearsden, where he would be required to spend four years – or so he thought.

If anything the atmosphere at St Peter's felt even more strained than at Blairs. There was clearly a certain distance between the staff and the student priests, which ran counter to the young man's natural affability. He recalled: "One of the things to do that's very important is that you must have friends. If you don't give any love to other people, and I don't mean sexual love – you won't get much of it back."

In 1945 the war ended. The young seminarian recorded his thoughts in a diary:

> "Victory Day, Tuesday 8 May 1945. Almost six years ago I sat at home and heard Mr N Chamberlain declare war on Germany. Today I sat in the common room of St Peter's College, Bearsden, in my first year of Theology and heard Mr W Churchill announce the unconditional surrender of the German forces. We have won the war; we have beaten Germany. The day which greeted the victor was a very dull one indeed. After breakfast the flags were put up on the front of the building. In pelting rain I went for a walk with Rev P McCusker and F Coyle to Milngavie to see the sights! We were soaked through, and arriving back shortly after noon we had to change almost all our clothing. Most of the afternoon was spent in Johnnie Cope's room and in the evening I made a holy hour before the Blessed Sacrament in thanksgiving for victory and in prayer for a just, charitable and Christian peace. I am now going to bed."

Vital building work was needed in the old college in Bearsden, and so in late October 1945 all the students were vacated to St Joseph's College, Mill Hill, on the outskirts of London. Tom's sense of dissatisfaction continued, however, as the strict rules laid down at St Joseph's did not allow for much in the way of enjoyment for free-spirited boys from working-class Lanarkshire!

Tom himself described the college as "tough going", and joined his classmates in close-knit conspiracies in how to bend if not break some of the less serious rules. These included a ban on visiting private homes, trying out the cafes in central London and even receiving food parcels from friends and family.

There was a welcome respite from the regime in 1945 when the students were permitted to go back home for Christmas.

The following year St Peter's, Bearsden, was destroyed by fire. The idea of going home, went up, quite literally, in smoke. Far from being the disaster it seemed, this event was to be the catalyst which was to bring the young Tom Winning face to face with the love of his life – the Church and city of Rome.

At the same time as St Peter's Bearsden was burning to the ground, the war's ending led to the reopening of Scots seminaries in Paris and Rome.

In October 1946 Tom joined twenty of his colleagues on a trip which was to have a major impact on his life. He was going to Rome. It was a city which had everything to enthral a young student priest.

The journey from Glasgow Central Station to the Eternal City involved a long trek across a Europe decimated by war. They endured a sometimes hazardous three-day train trip, as some of the bridges they crossed were of an unstable and temporary nature.

During a stopover in Paris they savoured the cosmopolitan flavour of the city's cafes and restaurants. It was late evening and it was also a time and a place for temptation: A heady cocktail. Tom admitted years later that it was here that he tasted wine for the first time in his life, though not he would concede, for the last!

The neon lights visible from the train windows seemed to come from another world for the young Scots who had grown accustomed to blackout curtains and candle-light illumination.

The Pontifical Scots College to which they were heading had been established in 1600 by Pope Clement VIII for Scots who, during the height of the Protestant Reformation, were denied the necessary training in their own country. Its initial *raison d'être* had been to provide a thorough education for all Catholic boys rather than as the exclusive preserve of trainee priests. However, sixteen years later the Pontiff decreed that it should be used to prepare men for working as priests on the Scottish Mission.

During the long and traumatic era of Catholic persecution in Scotland, the College was responsible for training a regular supply of clergy to support the Church back home in Scotland. In doing so, the Scots College played an integral part in preserving the faith in Scotland, and ensuring its embers were not extinguished completely.

On a spiritual level Rome promised the most enriching experience any trainee priest could wish for. It was the place which as a young boy Tom had read about, listened intently to visiting clergy talk about, and dreamed of seeing. Now he was there. The only other student from his year was Hugh McEwan.

Till his dying day, Tom Winning never knew why he and Hugh had been chosen to study in Rome. There was no apparent pattern to the placements. He knew no Italian, though his Latin was good. He had never dared dream of the move. In later life he simply said that apart from the gift of the faith and his family, the opportunity to study in Rome was the greatest privilege of his life.

Joining him in the seminary were postgraduate Jimmy McShane, men with late vocations, such as Felix Beattie, a former soldier and Stan Smith who had been a miner. The group, who bonded easily during the seventy-two hour trip, also included a man who was to become a close colleague and friend to Tom, the future Bishop Charles *Donny* Renfrew.

They were welcomed by the Rector William Clapperton, who had been assigned his post in 1922, but had been forced to flee the city during the wartime occupation.

Tom adapted to his third seminary in five years very easily indeed. Ironically the boy from Lanarkshire felt far more at home in Rome than in Bearsden or London.

Although he had never holidayed abroad before and was unaccustomed to sampling foreign cultures he displayed an aptitude for absorbing new experiences. He made friends with a young Hungarian called Josef Bistyo from the German-Hungarian College. Josef had been conscripted into the German army, but escaped to Rome to pursue his dream of becoming a priest.

Time off with fellow students in Rome.

Tom in St Peter's Square 1947.

Eager to strengthen his proficiency in Latin, Tom would chat with his new friend in the language of the Church and later claimed that these conversations helped him progress academically, since all lectures at the Gregorian University were in Latin.

His instinctive sociability was somewhat curtailed by the fact that seminarians were forbidden to take part in Roman nightlife. Visits to theatre, cinema, or even football matches were not permitted. And for a dedicated soccer fan, who continued from afar to follow the fortunes of Glasgow Celtic, this must have been a difficult rule to follow.

La Dolce Vita came to an abrupt end, however, when he was taken to hospital suffering from a small duodenal ulcer. He told doctors he had felt some discomfort weeks before leaving Scotland for Rome, but that he was reluctant to disclose it, fearing his lifetime ambition to study for the priesthood might be thwarted by ill health.

Cutting a dash in soup plate hats!

Post-war rationing in Italy had also added to his health problems as it became impossible to enjoy a healthy, balanced and full diet when food was scarce and meals were meagre.

Fortunately, the illness did not seem to have any noticeable effect on his studies. In addition to honing his skills in Latin there were daily theology classes at the Jesuit-run Gregorian University, where Tom and his friend Hugh McEwan enjoyed both the lessons and the chat.

It was perhaps a portent of things to come, however, that when Tom himself was given the opportunity to voice his opinions on moral philosophy he took a rather unconventional and independent line. When the seminarians were asked if it was ever allowable to cheat the system, every student said no – save one: Tom Winning. He reasoned that extreme poverty made it justifiable. "If your children are going hungry, if you get to the stage of extreme hunger, anybody's property becomes yours, because you have a right to survive. You can break into a bread van and steal a loaf. It would not be immoral to do that," he wrote.

His conviction was based on first-hand experience of poverty. Money in Rome, was in short supply. The Scots College was struggling to find its financial feet after its enforced closure, and the students were encouraged to shop around for the best bargains, careful to avoid the black market economy which had prospered during the war and its immediate aftermath.

An occasional treat involved making use of one of the fine restaurants outside the walls of Rome.

Though he would have loved to come home during the holidays, such indulgences were out of the question in the late 1940s. So, during the summer, the students were able to live in a

Tom at Scots College Villa, Marino 1948.

small villa and vineyard at Marino, outside Rome, which the Scots College had acquired in the seventeenthth century.

Another treat was to wander through Rome's cultural treasure trove. Just a year before he died he took advantage of the Jubilee Pilgrimage to revisit some of the wonderful tiny baroque Churches he remembered as a student. He recalled with fondness the location of a barber who did a good haircut for a handful of lire and enjoyed once more the street life of the eternal city – bantering with fruitsellers, chatting to children and visiting the Forum and Colisseum like any other tourist.

Because theatre-going was off-limits to the students it was agreed that they could stage their own performances within the building, where they had a small theatre. In addition to productions at Christmas and Lent they also staged Gilbert and Sullivan operas and Shakespeare plays, in which Tom played roles in many of them.

The all-male make up of the Scots College presented them with a potential problem: How would they cover the female roles? In stepped a very reluctant Tom Winning to steal the show. His appearances as Lady Macbeth, Ophelia and Calpurnia have not been forgotten! Though to his dying day he was still mortified at having to go into a Roman chemist, dressed in clerical soutane, to ask for nail-polish remover after the show!

The Cardinal often recalled that he never knowingly missed an opportunity to see Pope Pius XII during all his time in Rome. In later life he was called, somewhat disparagingly, a *Pope's man*. To the young student and the elderly Cardinal, such an epithet was a compliment.

That loyalty to Pius XII manifested itself six decades later when he defended the wartime Pontiff from charges that he had been anti-semitic.

In a lecture delivered just a year before he died, he recalled: "In the weeks leading up to the declaration of World War II Pius XII's efforts at dissuading the potential opponents from conflict became ever more insistent, culminating in his famous appeal, *'Nulla e' perduta con la pace, tutto lo puo' essere con la guerra'."* (Nothing is lost with peace, everything can be lost with war.) In the year 2000, he contacted the Jesuit priest in Rome who was preparing the beatification cause for Pius XII, offering his help in defending the reputation of the wartime Pope.

Tom, by now nearing the end of his studies in Rome, had cause to be grateful. Despite suffering periodic bouts of illness and homesickness he had grappled with the tutorials and examinations, all the while soaking up the cultural experiences. He was also, at twenty-three, a year younger than the age specified for ordination. It took the express permission of the Holy See to allow him to progress to ordination on 18 December, 1948.

Deacon Tom (left) at St John Lateran's Basilica.

His father sold his confectionery-making equipment to finance the family trip to Italy, where his parents, sister, uncles and aunts met the object of their pride outside the Basilica of St John Lateran, the Mother Church of the City of Rome and the world and the Pope's Cathedral.

The young student had originally been assigned another Roman Church for his ordination, but appealed to be allowed to receive the priesthood in the Mother Church of all Christendom. His request was granted.

At 1pm on that cold but bright ordination day he embraced once more his parents and family, after more than two years apart. Now it was they who called him *Father*.

Following his ordination Father Winning was assigned as curate at St Aloysius, Chapelhall, Lanarkshire. The

A college walk to the Spanish Steps.

parish, near Airdrie, had eight hundred parishioners, and it was ripe for the enthusiasm of a new man with fresh ideas. Fr Tom had no shortage of those.

The Winning family in Rome, December 1948.

He had a vision of where the Church should be in the parishes and on the wider national stage. He said, "The Catholic Church did not count. The conscience of the country rested with the Church of Scotland. We kept our heads down below the parapet. I felt there was something not right about that. I wanted the Church to be able to speak out in a prophetic way in society."

He made an early impression on the parish priest, Father Peter Murie, by his work with the Youth Club, the Union of Catholic Mothers and the Young Men's Society.

There were also signs that the dashing twenty-three year old, whom locals loved for the shine he brought home to them from Rome, would cause quite a stir in the locality. He was asked years later whether the presence of a young, handsome figure in the parish might have posed problems.

He replied: "It might be good not to be too conscious of the fact that you have things that would attract people. If you fancied yourself, you would revel like a peacock. When I look back I think that God must have been good to me. He gave me lots to do and to be. You grow into the role and you know the boundaries.

"It was easier for me as a young priest than it would be for many of them today because there was more reserve. People saw you as a person apart and they were taught to do that."

There were some difficult learning curves, however, along the way. Theory and study could not adequately prepare him for the harsh reality of ministering to people at the lowest point in their lives.

When he was called upon to make visits to the sick and administer the Last Rites to the dying, he struggled to remain composed and dispassionate

Ordination day December 18 1948.

from the emotion of the moment. He knew that these services to his people were the most important gifts he could bestow on them.

When the time came for Tom to leave the Parish and return to Rome, Father Murie, who suffered from various illnesses, gave a glowing report of his curate's help and support during his year-long stay.

The next step in Tom's ongoing education in Rome was to study Church or Canon Law. This included the rules governing ecclesiastical burial, sacraments, and issues surrounding marriage.

Tom felt sad to be leaving a parish he become attached to, doing the kind of work he had always wanted to do. Being back in Lanarkshire again had also allowed the chance to spend time with his parents and sister Margaret. He returned to his beloved Rome with a certain excitement and renewed enthusiasm for acquiring the knowledge of Canon Law which would hopefully make him a better priest when he came back to Scotland.

When he and his companions reached the Scots College again the familiar face of their friend Charles *Donny* Renfrew welcomed them. Hugh McEwan, Tom's only colleague from his year group at St Peter's to be sent to Rome with him had also come back to the Eternal City after serving as a priest in Glasgow.

Enjoying a spot of Roman cuisine!

These reunions with men from his previous period in Rome helped Tom to enjoy the familiarity of the surroundings which he had left behind. There was little time, however for socialising, as the lessons began in earnest almost immediately.

Tom's approach was not to criticise or pick holes in the laws he studied, but rather to seek to understand them better. An indication of his thinking at the time was revealed some years later when he was questioned about his unswerving loyalty to the doctrines of the Church.

He said: "The Church was given a mandate to interpret the word of God, assisted by the Holy Spirit, and not to conform to the fashions of the age. If you marry the fashions of the age, you'll be widowed before very long."

Tom's course lasted three years one of which was spent mainly completing his doctoral thesis. It was hard and unrelenting work.

Again his health seemed to give out, and after being forced to take a taxi to the examination hall, he went straight to bed for a full ten days, confined by a debilitating form of rheumatism. It was yet another health setback, but thankfully, one month's treatment alleviated the discomfort for all time.

The illness had taught Tom another valuable lesson: that over-reaching himself at the expense of his health was not only dangerous but counter-productive. How could he expect to be of service to the Church when he was pushing himself beyond the limit of his physical and mental endurance?

His health problems had not gone unnoticed by the church authorities. The Spiritual Director of the Scots College, Father Denis Meechan, had told him after his return to the city: "I was sure that you were never going to see your ordination. I thought you were going to die!"

In his second year he learned to pace himself, and as a result his health and his studies improved. Tom's thesis for the doctorate in Canon Law was a study of tithes in Scotland and, given his developing interest in past centuries, its basis was both canonical and historical.

Prior to returning to Rome after his summer in Scotland he researched documents and charters relating to Scottish abbeys in Glasgow's Baillie Institute.

The final examination for Tom's doctorate required him to undertake a forty-five minute lecture in Latin in front of five eminent professors on a subject of his choice. If ever there was a circumstance to set off his stomach ulcer again it was surely this. But diligent planning and preparation ensured that he not only succeeded, but *Doctor* Winning passed *cum laude*.

There was no time for a formal graduation ceremony, however, as he was instructed to take up a new post immediately: that of curate at St Mary's Church in Hamilton. His new post would also involve putting into practice his new skills, processing appeals for marriage annulments in the diocese of Motherwell.

Father Hamilton, the parish priest of St Mary's, knew Tom fairly well, having worked with him previously in St Patrick's. There were two fellow curates at the Church for the new boy to learn from: Fathers John Boyle and John Murray. Learn he did! Both were conscientious and hard working, often bearing the brunt of the parish work while Father Hamilton, in the traditional manner of Parish Priests of the time, remained somewhat aloof.

Before long he also had the company of a man who was to have a profound effect on his life and career in the future, Monsignor Gerry Rogers.

Their paths crossed when Edward Douglas, the Bishop of Motherwell, retired and was replaced by Bishop James Donald Scanlan, who moved from the diocese of Dunkeld and took over the offices of Gerry Rogers, the Vicar General. As a result the Monsignor resided with Tom and his colleagues at their parish house. The kindly cleric was to play a vital part in the Thomas Winning story.

Tom had not been home to see his parents since the summer of 1952, and was shocked to discover that his mother had been suffering from a tumour for almost a year. His parents were reluctant to inform him of the fact lest it interfere with his studies.

When he finally did discover the truth, it hit him all the harder. He immediately booked an appointment with a specialist, who told the family there was nothing that could be done. Ten months later she was dead. It was a bitter blow for the twenty-nine year-old, who had been close to his mother, and knew how proud she had been of him and his sister, Margaret. His mother's death was Fr Tom Winning's first intimate confrontation with death and bereavement.

Throughout this time, Tom was settling into St Mary's and proved a popular and well-respected asset to the parish. Encouraged by Bishop Scanlan, who had a high regard for the Boy Scout movement, Tom recruited over thirty scouts in St Mary's, and also qualified as a Scout Leader complete with the famed *wood-badge*.

He understood the dilemmas facing so many families in the Catholic community, and tried to assure them that allowing God a central place in their lives was a necessity. His mission, as he saw it, was to show people that Christ was not an optional extra to be added on to their lives on Sunday mornings but a living reality to be known, loved and served in their daily life.

When the time came for Monsignor Rogers to transfer to the duties of Administrator at Motherwell Cathedral, Tom was sorry to see him go. However, the parting was not to be long-lasting. Bishop Scanlan's next decision was to move Tom to the Cathedral in 1957 as Diocesan Secretary. However, his stay at the Cathedral was to last only twelve months. His new responsibility: to become the chaplain at the Franciscan Convent in Bothwell, Lanarkshire, a duty he could combine with his office role.

Home was now a secluded three-roomed house, with no housemates. It was an unwelcome departure from his customary living arrangements. Since childhood he had been accustomed to living in a busy, noisy house. It took quite a bit of getting used to.

Tom's very first task as chaplain to the sisters was to offer Mass for them. Added to this was the requirement to celebrate Mass for the pupils who attended their private school. This, coupled with Marriage Tribunal work and duties as Diocesan Secretary meant there was little time to get lonely.

His chosen life of celibacy, was lived with total naturalness. Later he would reflect: "There's no doubt it's a sacrifice. Mothers make many sacrifices for their children and I'm prepared to make sacrifices for Jesus Christ, for the Church. The rewards are great freedom of movement and disposal of your time. I've never dwelt on the fact that I don't have a family because I am close to many families."

The experience of coping with diocesan business was a valuable learning curve for Tom. He also discovered that living in the shadow of the enigmatic Scanlan had its difficulties. The good Bishop was a perfectionist, who would supervise every last detail of the administration Tom was working on.

His presence was larger than life and priests who were forced to face him without the obligatory written appointment were nervous before such a meeting.

Stories of his occasional outbursts of temper were legendary and, in his quest for reaching the highest standard for the diocese, he could be an exasperating and demanding boss.

His motivation, though, was admirable. He wanted to establish the Church and Catholic identity as a credible and powerful force in the Motherwell area. As Scotland was approaching the 1960s, the pace of life may have been changing, but some old habits were still depressingly extant. Sectarian division was particularly strong in Lanarkshire, where entire villages could be delineated along religious lines.

Even towns such as Airdrie and Coatbridge were known to have a preponderance of one faith in the area, with little or no social mix or interaction. Social problems and high unemployment played a part in fermenting the divisions. A journalist at the time remembered walking through a council estate in Lanarkshire at the height of the Orange marching season. He was confronted with graffiti which spelled out the message: *No Pope Here!* Underneath the caption someone had added: *Lucky Pope!*

It was in the midst of this environment that Bishop Scanlan, Father Winning and his associates at the diocese struggled to raise the profile of the Church, its activities and its teaching. To this end, the Bishop saw himself as a civic leader in the wider community. He realised that the higher the public profile of the bishop the more attention would be given to the message of the Church.

This strategy would make a profound impression on his young, observant, Diocesan Secretary. The similarities between Scanlan's approach and the one later adopted by Archbishop and Cardinal Winning are very clear.

It was supported by the basic belief that the only way that a minority religion and community could achieve confidence and status was by raising its head above the parapet. It could no longer be permissible for the Catholic community to crouch quietly on the sidelines, hoping that by keeping silent it might be overlooked and even tolerated.

It was the role of the clergy and Church hierarchy to lead this new era of self-renewal and advancement.

In this Tom could not have wished for a stronger or more inspiring teacher than James Donald Scanlan.

From Scanlan's point of view, Tom Winning was a valuable and important investment. No one could fail to recognise the enthusiasm and diligence which the Diocesan Secretary had displayed.

The year 1959 saw Monsignor Rogers nominated as a judge of the Roman Rota, the Catholic Church's Supreme Court dealing with marriage cases. It was a blow for Fr Winning to lose his mentor and friend. But a bigger blow was to follow almost immediately.

Thomas Winning senior was struck down by a fatal cerebral haemorrhage. It was a shocking blow which left Fr Tom reeling, struggling to comprehend the fact that he had now lost both his parents. He had never lost his sense of appreciation for the guidance and sacrifices which his parents made for himself and his sister.

His father's death, allied to overwork, brought on another breakdown in his own delicate health. The ulcer which first plagued him over fifteen years before erupted again and in 1960 he suffered a haemorrhage.

After being given time to recover from the illness he was given another dramatic change of role. He was named Spiritual Director at the Scots College in Rome. He was shocked at the news. He later confided to friends: "I would have thought they would have given me any role except that one. I always thought spiritual directors had to be exceptionally holy, always praying, almost mystics. I was far too practical."

In fact it was that no-nonsense spirituality, well integrated into a disciplined lifestyle which made him a fine role model for students and a popular spiritual director.

The college rector, Monsignor Flanagan, had specifically requested his appointment and Bishop Scanlan had agreed, with the proviso that Tom continue with his canon law studies while in Rome.

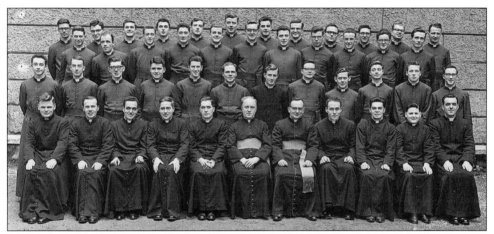

Scots College 1961. Fr Tom, Spiritual Director, is 5th from left, front row.

It was nine years since he had been in Rome and this time he was in a supervisory position. No longer was he the eager, but often carefree student. Now he was in a position responsible for the spiritual welfare of young student priests.

Although excited by the opportunity to work in the College, he was still struggling to come to terms with the death of his father, and he was a long way from his sister back home. Margaret had gone to University and become a teacher. She had also married and had two children: Agnes in 1956, and Edward two years later. Uncle Tom was enjoying being around the young family.

All of this was left behind as he knocked on the door of the old College in *Via Quattro Fontane* to present himself for duty. But far from throwing himself into intense activity, he fell straight into bed upon arrival.

He had been experiencing severe stomach problems for over a year. He was taken quickly to hospital. The ulcer which had plagued him before was removed, along with a sizeable section of his stomach.

The surgery was unexpected and serious. It necessitated a lengthy period of recuperation, and so it was that he spent the winter of 1961 and early spring of 1962 not in the panting heart of Rome, but in the care of the Blue Nuns at Fiesole, near Florence.

Later he recalled to a friend: "I wondered why God brought me there? I had studied so much, worked so hard, and wanted more than anything to go home and work in a parish in Lanarkshire. Yet here I was sitting on a lovely terrace in a villa overlooking Florence, eating bland puddings and drinking milky drinks!"

The doctors – and more especially the nuns – were taking no chances with the determined young Scot. Despite his protestations his recuperation was lengthy. When he finally received permission to go back to Rome, the purple drapes covered the statues of the eternal city, and the dramatic liturgies of Holy Week were being celebrated in every baroque basilica.

So it was that at Easter 1962 – six months after arriving – Fr Winning took up his duties as Spiritual Director of the *Pontificio Collegio Scozzese*.

Fortunately, the work involved Tom being more or less his own man. He had the remit of offering counselling, support and guidance to the students in a direct and confidential way. But far from waiting for them to come to him, Tom took the job a step further. He adopted a pro-active approach and formulated new ways of encouraging contemplation and prayer among the men.

The position was also of benefit to the Spiritual Director himself. He had the chance to re-examine his own attitude towards vocation. Escaping from the cumbersome tasks assigned him in Motherwell he could now devote more time than in the past to contemplation, reading and thought. He also benefited from his relatively light workload to explore further the city he had always loved.

He proved to be popular with staff and students alike. This was due largely to his relaxed and informal style of mixing with them. Previous seminarians, himself included, remembered the conditions at the Scots College could be rather regimented and constricted. This was not Winning's way, and he quickly established a reputation for a direct, but unpretentious manner in his dealings with everyone, whatever their rank or title.

He wrote, a few years later, in a remarkably frank and lyrical passage: "God gives us all some talents and expects us to use them in His service. We may be rich or poor, young or old, honoured or slighted, and it ought to affect us no more, neither to elate or depress us, than if we were actors in a play. They know that though they may appear to be superior to one another, to be prelates or peasants, they are, in reality, all on a level. The one desire which should move us should be, first of all, that of serving Him who endowed us with varying gifts, and of ensuring that our hands are full when we eventually go to meet Him."

His health began to improve steadily, and he found the time to take up golf again, although he only managed to view one football match.

He also used his time in Rome to study to become an advocate in the prestigious Sacred Roman Rota – the highest court in the Catholic Church for dealing with cases of nullity in marriage. This involved a few hours of classes every week, and a great deal of reading.

His Latin was fully tested, until he began to even think in the language of the Church. The final exams were the most stringent he had ever experienced during his vocation, and tend to dispel the future Cardinal's modest claim that he was not a serious academic. If he wasn't, he must have been an incredibly hard worker!

One test involved a written paper lasting twelve hours, with no meal breaks – and candidates were required to peruse an entire marriage case in Latin, translating statements into Italian and French. Of course he passed.

Now an Advocate of the Sacred Roman Rota, he was quickly put to work. Besides his continued duties at the Scots College, he was expected to devote some time each week to the service of the Rota. His old friend Monsignor Gerry Rogers was now a respected Judge there, and he asked his young protege to act as Notary in some high profile cases. Thus it was the Fr Tom took evidence in cases like that of Jackie Kennedy's sister, Lee Radziwill.

Back at the College life was far from settled. The building in the *Quattro Fontane* was deteriorating. Much work would have had to be done to upgrade the site, but the cost of renovation caused the Scottish bishops to rebuild on the (then) quieter area of the *Via Cassia* on the outskirts of Rome.

For two years, while the new college was being built, the staff and seminarians were required to reside at the villa in Marino, some distance from Rome.

Meanwhile the Church itself was beginning a period of upheaval.

Fr Tom's time in Rome had coincided with the pontificate of Pope, now Blessed John XXIII and the convocation of the Second Vatican Council.

Shortly after assuming office in 1958 the elderly "caretaker Pope" announced that there would be an ecumenical council – the first since 1870. It was to herald a remarkable era of reform, which would build on the pioneering changes brought about by his predecessor Pius XII.

John XXIII summoned 3,500 bishops and heads of religious orders to Rome in October 1962, and so it was that Fr Tom took on a new responsibility – looking after nine Scottish bishops who attended the sessions – all held in secret and conducted in Latin – within St Peter's Basilica.

Of course the strictures on secrecy quickly broke down. Journalists reported with great accuracy what was being said inside the Council. Fr Tom, was careful never to pry in his dealings with the bishops, but he developed a deep interest in the developments being proposed.

Among the items on the agenda were the role of the laity, reform of the liturgy, dealings with other religions, the Church and the media and the Church's role in the modern world.

The Scottish bishops were disadvantaged by the use of Latin in the debates. Although expert enough at liturgical Latin, their shaky grasp of the spoken language meant they found it difficult to make quick and decisive contributions. If only they had been able to take in the young Fr Winning with them to express their views in *lingua latina* . . .

The reactions to the Council of the Bishops of Scotland were varied. They felt neither comfortable in the traditionalist camp comprised mostly of Italian, Irish and American bishops, nor the liberal wings from Holland, France and Germany.

Fr Tom was not allowed to attend the Council's formal sessions – such occasions were the sole preserve of the Bishops. But he attended the daily talks and discussions by theologians as a college staff member and, when the bishops asked him to be their canon law consultant at their Scots College conferences, he acted as Minute Secretary and discovered much more about the great debates.

It is difficult to over-estimate the long-term impact the Second Vatican Council deliberations had on the young priest.

When he became a parish priest in Motherwell, he eagerly set about putting the Council's directives into action. He delighted in pioneering lay readers, discussion groups and the vernacular liturgy. As Archbishop, his vision was unashamedly that of creating a "Church of Vatican II".

The whirlwind that was the Council was still being felt forty years later when the then Cardinal Winning died. Its insights were still being discovered, and his appetite to put its vision into place was every bit as great as it had been in those halcyon days in Rome in the early 1960s.

Meanwhile, back home in Scotland the Church was changing too.

During the five years he had been away in Rome as Spiritual Director of the Scots College, James Donald Scanlan had become Archbishop of Glasgow and the new Bishop of Motherwell, Frank Thomson called Tom back to become Parish Priest of St Luke's Church in Motherwell in 1966.

He was absolutely delighted. It was to this work that he had felt called as a child; it was the thought of working with people in the parish which had sustained him in his long years of study. He believed, quite genuinely, that his career on the clerical ladder was over – and he couldn't have been happier.

The parish was small in number but social problems loomed large. Poor housing, unemployment and low income combined to produce a community in Forgewood with an abundance of no-go areas. It was a challenge to minister to the needs of the practising Catholics in the area. Even more difficult was appealing to the significant number of lapsed Catholics who did not attend weekly Mass. It was a challenge Fr Winning relished.

Tom's belief was that for the parish to survive and prosper it was imperative to nurture the young. He encouraged boys with little or no connection to the Church to become altar boys. Girls were given roles in the offertory procession and asked to read from scripture.

Shortly after taking up residence in St Luke's he requested permission from the bishop to say Mass facing the parishioners, and also experimented with the new funeral and baptismal services.

First Communion Day, Motherwell 1967.

In embracing these initiatives Tom was perceived as a liberal priest. However, in the social climate of the times, the "never had it so good" era of the permissive and materialist 1960s, Father Winning held no brief for the prevailing values sweeping Scotland.

He looked on in anguish as family life came under fierce attack from the "progressive" thinkers of the age. He agonised over the thousands of the faithful drifting from the Church over Pope Paul's *Humanae Vitae* with its teaching on artificial birth control. Later he was to define that encyclical "prophetic" since it predicted many of the negative consequences of the swinging sixties.

Tom had the opportunity to explore these issues further as he remained Minute Secretary at the Bishops' meetings and was in the rare position of knowing the Bishops personally and being trusted by them.

He had also kept open the channels he had established in Rome and these factors conspired to see Tom assigned the role of Vicar Episcopal in his diocese, with special responsibility for marriage.

He took to this new post with the same energy that had characterised his studies.

Preparing a young family for baptism.

Introducing young readers at Mass, 1969.

After launching courses for lay Catholics and Sunday Evening Services which attracted over two hundred people, he started a Parish Council, and such visible success led to Scotland's bishops asking him to produce a paper on the establishment of a National Marriage Tribunal.

The paper was all too persuasive, and in 1970 Tom was called to put his ideas for a national marriage tribunal into action by becoming its founding president. The tribunal was to be based in Glasgow, the largest diocese in Scotland. This meant that Fr Tom had to move out of his beloved Lanarkshire once more to take up residence in the "dear green place".

The move saw Fr Tom team up once more with his long-time mentor Archbishop Scanlan. The Archbishop of Glasgow had made quite a mark not only on the Church, but on Scottish public life. Almost twenty new parishes had been established, with seven new churches and a new centre of religious education built. In addition nine more religious orders came into the archdiocese. It was an admirable track record. Yet at the age of seventy-two he was conscious that the work of implementing Vatican II had to be carried out by a younger man with fresh energy and ideas.

Corpus Christi Day Procession, Motherwell 1969.

There was so much work involved in his new role at the recently established National Marriage Tribunal that Tom gave little thought to the succession to Scanlan. He certainly harboured no ambition for the role, casually remarking that, "the man who gets that job will have his life shortened by a decade at least!"

In mid-October of that year he received a message to call the Apostolic Delegate, Archbishop Domenico Enrici in London. It was to be a conversation which astonished Tom, and would alter his life and career dramatically. The archbishop said: "The Holy Father would like you to accept the post of Auxiliary Bishop to the Archbishop of Glasgow."

An on-the-spot answer was required, but it was an offer he couldn't refuse. The Church needed him. The senior clergy who had nominated him knew his ability to apply single-minded dedication to his pastoral work, and his natural ease with people around him would prove a valuable asset.

Episcopal ordination, St Andrew's Day 1971: (Left to right) Bishop Stephen McGill, Bishop Tom Winning, Archbishop James Donald Scanlan, Cardinal Gordon Gray, Bishop Francis Thomson.

Tom wasn't so sure. It wasn't false modesty which made him doubt himself, but the enormity of the task involved. Nevertheless, on St Andrew's Day 1971 the new 'Auxiliary Bishop of Glasgow and Titular Bishop of Louth' received the mitre and crozier in a ceremony held in St Andrew's Cathedral in Glasgow's Clyde Street. There was no sense of personal satisfaction, just a readiness to serve the Church as the Church wanted to be served.

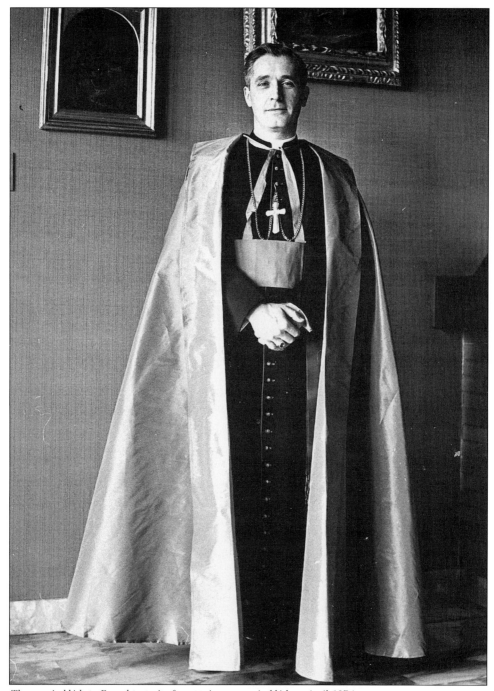

The new Archbishop: Formal portrait after appointment as Archbishop, April 1974.

Shortly after his ordination he began to tour the diocese, staying at a different parish each weekend, meeting parishioners and priests, visiting school children and the sick and aged.

It was particularly important to him not to lose contact with the grass roots Catholic community in its widest sense. It also had the added effect of making him a well-known and accessible figure.

Before long, however, Archbishop Scanlan persuaded Bishop Winning to take over the parish of Our Holy Redeemer's in Clydebank, after the sudden death of the priest there. Tom was uneasy about the dual-role and resolved to concentrate on his duties as bishop, delegating parish administration to his curates, and continuing with his tours.

On 21 October 1973 Tom was informed that Bishop James Ward, the senior Auxiliary Bishop in Glasgow had suffered a fatal heart attack. A few months later, Achbishop Scanlan announced his retirement.

Speculation within the Archdiocese centred on his successor. Tom Winning hoped it would be Monsignor Gerry Rogers, his friend from Rome. Indeed, he had written in a requested memo to the Apostolic Delegate that the Monsignor was the Archbishop Glasgow needed.

Shortly afterwards Bishop Tom was called to a meeting in London by the new Apostolic Delegate, the Swiss prelate Bruno Heim. Assuming he would be asked to expand on his memo, Tom left with a full dossier on the merits of Mgr Rogers. On arrival, he was simply asked to put his homework aside.

Archbishop Heim calmly stated that Thomas Joseph Winning would be the next Archbishop of Glasgow. No one could have been more surprised than the man himself.

He adopted as his personal motto: *Caritas Christi urget nos*, Christ's love urges us on. This was reflected in his first homily delivered at his installation at St Andrew's when he declared. "Every generation has its own contribution to make to Christ's work, a contribution which can be made by no other. What has to be done now has to be accomplished by us or it will never be done at all." It was to prove to be more than heady rhetoric for a historic moment.

The new archbishop had a clear agenda. As warm and personable as he was, those closest to him knew that he could just as easily employ an iron fist within the velvet glove. Asked to describe his own attributes as a boss, he replied, "Quite demanding" and conceded that "a bad temper" was one of his failings.

His first meeting with the Glasgow priests was notable for skipping the pleasantries. He had called them for a purpose: to discuss plans for the future and set out his personal vision. He stated that he wanted all his priests to attend a month-long refresher course at the Scots College, Rome to receive lectures on Vatican II.

He also covered the subjects of the archdiocesan finances and constructive criticism from the clergy. And, should there be any doubt over his views on religious education. He told them: "There is pressure from outside to integrate Catholic schools. As far as I'm concerned it would not be integration but disintegration if that happens because we would be integrating with nothing!"

One of Archbishop Winning's first initiatives was to appoint fourteen priests to assume control of various areas including Justice and Peace, Youth and communications. These men would be responsible for moving such issues forward, and encouraging active involvement from their parishioners.

On the issue of inter-church relations, Tom believed that actions spoke louder than words. So when an invitation was received from the Church of Scotland to speak at their General Assemby in 1975, the first to a Roman Catholic Archbishop, Tom accepted. Despite opposition from some sections within the Kirk, Tom's historic address was received warmly by the Assembly delegates, and marked a genuine turning point in ecumenical affairs in Scotland.

Adopting the dress code sported by the assembled ministers, a black frock-coat, Tom asked the question which would break the four hundred year silence between the two Churches. "What do brothers say to one another after years, and in our case centuries, of estranged silence? Surely they ask forgiveness."

Thanking the Kirk for its invitation, he reaffirmed his Church's commitment to seeking dialogue and reconciliation with their separated brethren. However, he added a caveat, "It's a rough road and there are stumbling blocks for all. We, for example, in the Roman Catholic Church, realise that we are a stumbling block to other churches because of our convictions regarding the nature of the Church and her authority."

It was a refreshingly honest appraisal of the relationship between both traditions, and pre-empted many of the themes Pope John Paul would develop twenty years later in his historic encyclical *Ut Unum Sint*.

The year 1976 was a time of mixed fortunes. The early part was over-shadowed by the sudden death of Archbishop Scanlan in London. Although seventy-five years old, he had just taken up the chaplaincy of a convent in the city. Archbishop Winning, ironically was also in London the day his predecessor died, attending the ordination of Abbot Basil Hume of Ampleforth as the new Archbishop of Westminster.

Later in the year another man who was soon to mould an era of his own came briefly into Tom's life. During a trip to a Eucharistic Congress in Philadelphia he first heard an imposing and impressive Polish Cardinal preach for a full hour without notes.

"Who's the Pole?" Tom asked one of his companions from the United States. "He's Karol Wojtyla, the young Archbishop of Cracow," came the reply. It was a name Tom was to hear again.

Back home, Tom's strong identification with the poor and disadvantaged began to manifest itself in his public pronouncements and actions. The experiences of his childhood and upbringing had remained with him, and now he was rapidly acquiring the power and influence which could help highlight the problems of poverty and social injustice.

One practical project was his decision in June 1977 to divert two million pounds intended to extend and renovate St Andrew's Cathedral into care services provided by the Church in Glasgow. He said at the time: "Glasgow is already the most deprived city in Britain; it follows, therefore, that we are the most deprived diocese. While proud of the work being carried out by so many organisations within the Church on behalf of the sick, the elderly and the handicapped, the young and the destitute, I look at the deprivation around us and ask, what is the Church doing about it?"

While conceding that a new and modern cathedral was required, he stressed: "I can't go ahead with a full-scale renovation when so many of our fellow citizens are suffering so much. The Church is concerned with the whole person and not merely the building of churches." It was an act which would come to typify the kind of ministry which he wanted for the Catholics of Glasgow. To aid his efforts at improving communication in the diocese, he began the publication of a monthly newspaper *Flourish*, which continues to this day.

As his profile within the city and the country grew he was also establishing his credentials internationally. Outspokenness had always been a hallmark of his career, and it would continue to be so in his role as archbishop. The difference was that now more and more people were listening.

The media were also becoming aware that his charismatic presence and natural way with words could be used to full effect when he had a specific point to make. When, in 1978, Pope Paul VI did not grant a dispensation to Baroness Maria Cristina Von Reibnitz, a Catholic, and Prince Michael of Kent, an Anglican, to be married in a Catholic Church, Prince Charles made a thinly veiled attack on the decision, and the "folly" of "Christians arguing about doctrinal matters".

Incensed by the remarks, Tom responded by accusing the Prince of advocating a "woolly" type of Christianity. He also suggested, not for the last time, that the royal might turn his attention to the Act of Settlement, which prohibits a Roman Catholic from becoming monarch.

The only member of the Catholic hierarchy in Britain to speak out, he received national television exposure and international headlines. Privately Tom felt extremely isolated. His remarks had not produced a single supportive comment from any of his fellow bishops. He was reassured, however by a friend in Rome who passed on word that Paul VI wished the Archbishop of Glasgow to know of his gratitude for the stance taken.

In 1978 the Church was to undergo a tumultuous time. The death of Pope Paul VI in August was followed by the election of Albino Luciani, the smiling Pope John Paul I, whose stewardship was to last a mere thirty-three days before his death due to heart failure.

The second Conclave of Cardinals that year resulted in the shock election of the first non-Italian Pope since the sixteenth century: Karol Wojtyla, the Archbishop of Cracow in Poland. This man, who so impressed Tom when he heard him speak in Rome in 1976, was now successor of St Peter and Supreme Pontiff of the Universal Church.

Almost immediately after his inauguration, Pope John Paul II let it be known that his papacy would not be confined to the walls of Vatican City. He soon acquired the title of *the travelling Pope*, and Tom, ever seeking new, ground-breaking initiatives, hoped that one of his foreign trips might include Scotland. In mid–1980 it was announced that a tour of Britain would take place in the summer of 1982.

The Catholic community in Scotland was overjoyed at the prospect and eleven committees were appointed, comprising over five hundred people, to prepare and organise the visit to Scotland.

Tom saw John Paul's visit as an opportunity to provide an impetus to the spiritual life in the Church in his country. If this historic event was to achieve far-reaching effects, then it had to involve and inspire the entire Catholic community, particularly those who had fallen away.

In May 1981, however, disaster struck. Crowds in St Peter's Square watched in horror as John Paul collapsed in pain, struck by two bullets fired at close range while he waved to pilgrims from his Popemobile. It was a scene which stunned the world and threw the planned visit into doubt.

Thankfully John Paul bounced back and the visit seemed on until violence once more intervened. On 2 April 1982 Argentina invaded the Falkland Islands, and immediately provoked a conflict with Britain's Thatcher Government.

How could the Pope visit a country waging war against a Catholic nation which was certain to regard such a trip as a slight?

Tom faced this new disappointment with a resolve which threw him into a leadership role once more. To him, the assassination attempt was an un-controllable obstacle to a papal visit, but war should not prevent the Vicar of Christ from coming to be among his people.

He would do everything he could to ensure that a way could be found to put the visit back on course. Tom began lobbying fellow bishops, Church groups and even the Argentine Cardinals to write to the Pope their fervent hopes for the *"pastoral and non-political"* visit to be given the go-ahead.

Two days later Archbishop Worlock of Liverpool called Tom and suggested they both go out to Rome and plead their case to the Pope himself. Clearing it with Cardinal Gordon Gray, Tom joined Worlock for a journey which would make or break the Papal Visit to Britain. The omens looked good. News reached the two at Heathrow Airport that the Holy Father had pencilled them in for lunch. It was an agonising one for Tom. Though tempted by the menu he dared not eat too much lest he be unable to say something pertinent because his mouth was full! A deal was struck. John Paul would visit Britian and follow up that visit with a quick tour of Argentina.

John Paul II arrived at Gatwick Airport on 28 May 1982, the first reigning Pope ever to set foot on British soil. Tom Winning was present among the dignitaries welcoming him. It wasn't yet Scotland, but the exasperated Archbishop could only breath a huge sigh of relief that the Pontiff was ever nearer his nation.

When he finally flew to RAF Turnhouse in Edinburgh there was much speculation amongst the crowd and commentators as to whether he would recognise Scotland's identity as a separate nation by kneeling and kissing its ground. He did so, and immediately, millions of Scots respected the gesture.

To the Catholic youth awaiting him in Murrayfield Stadium, respect and euphoria were intermingled. "John Paul II We Love You," they cried. "Young people of Scotland, I love you!" boomed back the Polish baritone. The sun-drenched joy of Murrayfield set the tone for the entire tour, which included an historic meeting with the Church of Scotland Moderator under the unyielding gaze of John Knox's statue, and a visit to the National Catholic Teachers' Training College, Notre Dame, in Glasgow's Bearsden.

The undoubted highlight of the two-day event was the Papal Mass at Bellahouston Park where over 300,000 gathered to cheer their spiritual leader in the glorious sunshine.

"Dearly beloved Catholics of Scotland," he told them amidst rapturous applause, "the prayers of your forefathers did not go unanswered – with grateful hearts turn to God and thank him that tranquil days have been restored to the Catholic community in Scotland."

During his homily the assembled throng cheered and sang, causing him to pause for over eight minutes. It was the emotional culmination of centuries of discrimination and marginalisation of a minority held in contempt. They had now come into their own, and their Pope was urging them to look forward as a self-confident, significant section of Scottish society.

When Tom accompanied John Paul in his ever-present *popemobile* around the park they cheered him louder still. It was a joyous and heartening day, but the Archbishop knew it was just the beginning of the effort to renew the Church's relationship with a declining membership. He had brought the Pope to his people in Scotland. Now he must strive to bring back his people to their Church.

Ever the raconteur, Tom Winning loved to recount the story of their con-versation in the vehicle as they toured the park. An improptu chorus of *Will ye no come back again* was echoing round the crowd and the Archbishop whispered to Pope, "It's a song about Bonnie Prince Charlie, Your Holiness."

"Ah, yes," said the Pope. "I met him in London earlier in the week . . ."

A renewal programme had been launched to prepare for the Papal Visit and now Archbishop Tom was determined to build on it so as to widen the active participation and involvement of lay Catholics. Over sixty per cent of Catholics did not attend Church and arresting this grim development weighed heavily on his mind.

The flock had acquired more material possessions, many felt too sophisticated and educated for the perceived simplicity of religion. There also existed a tendency to practise *à la carte* Catholicism, with many adherents preferring to pick and choose aspects of the doctrines they felt comfortable with. More worryingly still for the Archbishop was that the young increasingly felt no blood-tie to their faith which their parents and grandparents did.

He stressed the road would be long and arduous and meant, "moving from a 'pray, pay and obey' kind of Church to one which is more concerned about unity within community and harnessing the gifts with which we are blessed."

Projecting his vision of the future was a task for which he needed the energy and commitment of all sections of the church: clergy, religious and laity. It had always been his contention that the economic and social problems which beset Glasgow helped prevent Catholics playing a full and productive part in the life of the church. Undertaking an extensive study of the root causes of apathy showed his instinctive feeling to be correct. He instigated Resource Teams and Pastoral Care Plans to tackle social problems.

Throughout the 1980s Archbishop Winning's status, and that of the Church, was rising and was reflected in his being awarded an Honorary Doctorate in Divinity at Glasgow University and the Loving Cup, a gift from the city of Glasgow in recognition of outstanding service.

In 1990 Archbishop Tom reached the age of sixty-five. He had seen many changes in the Church over the years. Some he had played a key role in implementing. Most men his age were retiring. For Tom Winning, the best was yet to come.

During the 1991 Gulf War Tom spoke out against the "unspeakable holocaust" he feared western military involvement would provoke in the Middle East. Although unpopular with some politicians and sections of the media his anti-war rhetoric and belief in diplomacy before destruction was consistent with the statements of John Paul II and the traditional Christian opposition to war. Glasgow Catholics flocked to Masses for Peace all over the city, each celebrated by their Archbishop.

He also found favour with the Scottish Muslim Community and was invited to Glasgow's Central Mosque to address them on the Middle East crisis.

He expressed further irritation that year accusing the Labour Party of allowing a "wave of persecution" against Pro-Life MPs and candidates and calling on Catholic voters to carefully consider politicians' pro-life record.

The public response from the Labour Party was a very deafening silence, yet privately there was much gnashing of teeth regarding the Archbishop's reluctance to remain out of the political arena. There was a failure to understand that on crucial matters of moral and ethical import, Tom regarded it as his duty to state uncompromisingly the Church's position.

He had done so during the Thatcher years, when he perceived the monetarist agenda was oppressing the poor and the less fortunate. His criticism would encompass all parties and policies which he felt were contrary to the betterment of society.

In 1993 the retired Cardinal Gray died, and the eighty-three year old's passing led to speculation that there might be a replacement Cardinal appointed in the future.

The Apostolic Nuncio, Archbishop Luigi Barbarito, the Vatican's representative in Britain sought to quash the rumours by pointing out that several years were likely to pass before a new intake of Cardinals, and a Scottish red hat was not guaranteed.

Tom himself stood away from the fray preferring to concentrate on his duties, which now included tackling a nine million pound Archdiocesan debt, which he had partly inherited and partly incurred and which soaring interest rates had helped increase. It was therefore with some surprise that Tom received a call in October 1994 from Archbishop Barbarito telling him that the Holy Father now wished his services as a Prince of the Church. Cardinal Winning would later describe the news as breathtaking.

Speculation had subsided after Barbarito's 1993 comments, and such was the secrecy surrounding the decision, the momentous announcement had an added and immense impact. Glasgow now had its first Cardinal in history and Scotland its second home-based red hat since the Reformation.

Asked to observe strict secrecy until the official announcement, the news reached congregations on the Sunday morning of 30 October 1994. They reacted by breaking into spontaneous applause, and messages of congratulations poured in from across Britain and abroad. Media coverage was extensive with Glasgow's *Herald* newspaper running the headline:

Scotland's status reinforced within the Catholic Church.

Much was made of Tom's life-long links with Rome, his conservative stance on theological issues and his skill for diplomatic manoeuvring, which although unlikely to see him elevated to the Papacy would secure him an influential place in determining Church policy, and the future Pope.

For the Catholic community in Scotland it was simply a joyous blessing which bestowed a special recognition of their contribution to building the faith against overwhelming odds.

The consistory ceremony took place on 26 November and over 1,500 Scots flew to Rome to support their new Cardinal.

He himself had gone out a week before to prepare, and travelled to Rome airport to personally welcome every well-wisher who arrived to see him admitted to the College of Cardinals. It was an electric atmosphere in Rome for those memorable five days.

The new Cardinal Winning was deeply moved by the ceremony when he received his scarlet biretta with the reminder that the colour symbolised the Cardinal's readiness to serve the Church *Usque ad effusionem sanguinis* – to the point of shedding his own blood for the Church. That phrase was a constant reminder to him in his last seven years of life that he had a duty to speak the truth in season and out of season, popular or unpopular.

Later Pope John Paul addressed the new Cardinal thus, "Cardinal Winning, as priest and bishop you have always been what is called *a man of the people* with great personal sensitivity for the welfare of the less fortunate." He ended with the stirring words, "May Saint Andrew and Saint Margaret, Scotland's patrons, and Saint Mungo, special patron of Glasgow, intercede for all the bishops, priests and laity of your beloved land."

The celebrations continued throughout the year, and on 11 December 9,000 people gathered in Glasgow 's Scottish Exhibition and Conference Centre to celebrate Mass with their new Cardinal. It was the beginning of a new era of peace and joy, which would last for an all-too-short period.

Roderick Wright, Bishop of Argyll and the Isles, went missing in September 1996. Previously the then Archbishop Winning, along with Keith O'Brien, Archbishop of St Andrews and Edinburgh had questioned Bishop Wright about allegations of an improper relationship with a woman. The Bishop had strenuously denied them.

Now, however, it emerged that not only had he fled his diocese with the woman, but the tabloids were set to reveal that he had a fifteen-year-old son from an earlier relationship.

When Bishop Roddy came for a secret face-to-face meeting with Cardinal Winning, he offered his resignation, and a disheartened Tom faced the press to announce that while the Church regretted Roddy Wright's departure, the door would remain open should he ever wish to return as a priest.

In an ideal world that should have been the end of the matter. However, the public and media appetite for more salacious revelations guaranteed that the biggest love scandal ever to hit Scotland, would keep Bishop Wright's transgressions, and Tom, fully in the public glare. The former bishop later sold his story to one of the tabloid newspapers.

Inevitably, questions were asked of the new Cardinal's involvement in the handling the situation. What did he know and when did he know of it? The truth was that accepting Wright's cast-iron denials of romantic affairs left him unable to pursue the matter further. In Cardinal Tom's code of ethics a prelate's word of honour carried great weight.

Moving to draw a line under the traumatic episode, the Cardinal responded to secular press intrusion by suggesting that they might put their own house in order before delving into the inadequacies of the Church and its rules on male, celibate priests. He compared some elements of the tabloids to the Gestapo, and admitted, "I still have good thoughts about him. I never felt resentment, just disappointment. I still have high hopes for big Roddy."

The biggest casualty of the controversy was the attention it diverted from the causes with which the Church were identified. The abortion issue was one which Tom intended to pursue as Cardinal every bit as much as he had as an archbishop, bishop and priest. Society was failing to safeguard the rights of the unborn, and words from the Church were insufficient. He believed that practical support was badly needed.

In a blaze of publicity in 1997 Cardinal Winning generated international attention by calling on women, Catholic and non-Catholic alike, who were contemplating an abortion to come to the Church for help. Cynics quickly dubbed it his *cash for babies* scheme, but in reality the Pro-Life Initiative was Tom's vision of practical Christianity made flesh.

The emphasis was on compassion allied to spiritual and financial support rather than condemnation. Its continued success can be measured by the fact that hundreds of thousands of pounds are still being contributed to the project four years after its launch.

Elsewhere the Cardinal's campaigns were to encompass both the sacred and the profane.

When the incoming Labour government reconvened Scotland's Parliament, Tom Winning harboured some hope that its legislative agenda would reverse many of the social injustices and inequalities which had plagued Scotland in recent years. His reaction was one of dismay when he learned that one of the first priorities of the new Lib-Lab coalition was the repeal of the legislation which banned the promotion of homosexuality in schools. The law, Section 2a of the 1986 Local Government Act (or Clause 28) had been described by the minister as having 'no place in the Scotland of tomorrow.'

Tom considered its removal to be a serious challenge to the stability of family life. His view was shared by Brian Souter, the devout Christian boss of the Stagecoach company who ran a privately funded referendum on the issue.

The battle generated much heat on both sides and Cardinal Winning became a hate figure for some gay rights groups who took offence at the stance of the Church. It hurt him deeply that his defence of the Church's position was perceived as bigoted. It horrified him even more that dissolute people might use his words to justify violence toward homosexual people. An article outlining his opposition to repeal was carried in *The Spectator,* which elicited a personal reply from Sir Elton John.

He spoke more in sorrow than anger when he said that the Church had never refused to minister to homosexuals, and resolutely maintained that gay people be treated with love and compassion.

When ballot papers were posted out to nearly four million people 1,260,846 papers were returned of which 1,094,440 were in favour of keeping the clause and 166,406 supported repeal.

It was clear that the Cardinal was more in touch with the feelings of most Scots on the issue than the politicians. However the Scottish Executive pressed on regardless, and scrapped the law.

Nevertheless a new and strict code of guidance was introduced to govern the teaching of sex education in schools, a clear bid by the new Parliament to address the fear of Cardinal Winning and many like him.

In the months just before he died, one issue so concerned Cardinal Winning that he said the previously unthinkable. In an article for the *Herald* newspaper he admitted he came close to feeling ashamed of his adopted home city of Glasgow.

The reason for his shame? The treatment of asylum seekers by a small but violent minority of people who had sought to use them as a scapegoat for the ills of their own communities. That persecution would culminate in the death of an asylum seeker some weeks later.

While most politicians fell uncharacteristically silent on the issue of accepting families fleeing political persecution, Cardinal Winning issued a statement saying: "It would take a lot to make me ashamed to say that I live and work in Glasgow. But the treatment meted out to asylum seekers in recent weeks comes close to bringing these words to be uttered."

He also condemned the "institutionalised discrimination," suffered by refugees and called for the scrapping of the voucher system and the unjust treatment of asylum seekers looking for work. He added: "How can the baptised claim to welcome Christ if they close the door to the foreigner who comes knocking?" That prophetic article was to be his last public statement.

On Friday 8 June 2001 Cardinal Winning was rushed to the intensive care unit at Glasgow's Victoria Infirmary Hospital after suffering a sudden heart attack on his way home from the Archdiocesan offices. The shock around the Catholic world was palpable.

Despite being seventy-six he had always retained a youthful vigour, and only three months earlier the Vatican agreed to appoint an auxiliary bishop to help him with the arduous task of running the Archdiocese of Glasgow.

The press carried prominent reports of his condition for the next few days, with the *Scottish Catholic Observer* headlining a personal message from Pope John Paul, which read:

> "Having learned of your illness I wish you to know that I am close to you in prayer at this time. I entrust you to the loving care of Our Lady and with affection I impart my Apostolic Blessing as a pledge of grace and peace in Our Lord and Saviour Jesus Christ."

Cards and messages flooded the hospital and prayers offered up for his recovery.

His diary was cleared for three months, and visitors to the hospital remarked on the Cardinal's almost childlike gratitude to staff and friends for their concern, together with his amazement that for the first time in his adult life he was to be free of official duties for a while.

Alas, his joy was to be short-lived. On Sunday 17 June, as he was getting out of bed, he suffered a massive and fatal heart attack. His devoted housekeeper, Mrs Isobel McInnes heard him fall and rushed to help him, but nothing could be done. It was at 12.30pm that fateful Sunday that a press conference was convened at the Archdiocesan Offices in Clyde Street. It fell to the Cardinal's closest collaborators to make the grim news public.

Mgr James Clancy, his long-time friend and Vicar General said simply: "It is my sad duty to inform you that Cardinal Winning died this morning."

Mgr Peter Smith, his chancellor and MC spoke of celebrating the last Mass at which the Cardinal assisted on earth less than twenty-four hours before his death and spoke of his "deep faith in God and God's love for him".

Ronnie Convery, the Archdiocesan spokesman said simply: "I heard him being asked how he would like to be remembered, and he replied, quick as a flash, 'I want them to say he had time for us.' As anyone who was privileged to know him will agree, he certainly did have time for us."

For a week the Cardinal's body lay in state, and thousands of mourners from all walks of life filed past to pay their repsects.

The Funeral Mass at St Andrews Cathedral heard him described by Bishop Joseph Devine of Motherwell as "a superstar of the Roman Catholic Church ." Yet for all his natural charisma and high position as Prince of the Church he remained in essence a priest of the people. Thousands gathered outside the Cathedral and applauded a casket containing the man who came to epitomise traditional Christianity in twenty-first century Scotland.

He was still one of their own.

He left behind a world very different from the one into which he had been born seventy-six years earlier, but a better world for having known the influence, the enthusiasm, yes, and the smile, of Thomas Joseph Cardinal Winning.

In the words of Yeats: "Tho' Much Is Taken, Much Abides."

Requiescat in pace.

FAREWELL

PRINCE OF THE CHURCH

I remember when he became a Cardinal I was present in Rome and heard the Holy Father speak of his extraordinary pastoral love and his great success in reaching out to his people. He was a great hero of mine and a great example and I will certainly miss him.

Cardinal Theodore McCarrick

Archbishop of Washington DC, USA

In November 1994, Cardinal Winning and myself were elevated to the College of Cardinals together. Our Holy Father offered us the opportunity for a joint audience for all those from English speaking nations. I remember vividly the huge number of pilgrims from Glasgow and their unbridled enthusiasm, deep love and obvious respect for our Holy Father Pope John Paul II as well as their beloved Thomas Cardinal Winning. I have no doubt that Cardinal Winning must have been a gentle and loving shepherd to have earned such respect and affection.

Cardinal Adam Maida

Archbishop of Detroit, USA

I remember when Cardinal Tom received the red hat in Rome, I was present when Pope John Paul called out all the names of the new cardinals and each received warm applause. But when he called out the name of Cardinal Tom Winning, the shout of joy and approval – well, it could have been Celtic scoring the winning goal!

There was a sense in which Cardinal Tom was, as St Augustine put it, "a bishop for them but, first of all, a Christian with them".

Cardinal Cormac Murphy O'Connor

Archbishop of Westminster

A solemn moment: Taking possession of St Andrew's Cathedral 1974.

A happy moment: visiting friend and colleague Bishop Mario Conti of Aberdeen.

Midnight Mass at a Glasgow parish: smiling through the sleet!

Our Holy Father, Pope John Paul II, has a talent for asking penetrating questions when they are least expected. When Cardinal Francis George, of Chicago, saw the Holy Father for his fifteen-minute chat in Rome, he was taken by surprise when he was asked, "How are you influencing the culture?"

As President of the Pontifical Council for Culture, I often ask myself that very question as I read through the reports which flood into my office from all over the world. Sometimes I am even able to ask bishops when they visit my office.

In Cardinal Winning's case, there is a very clear answer. The prophets of doom thought he was unrealistic and possibly mad when, in March 1997, he took the bold step of offering practical help to women from any religious, social or racial background, who felt under pressure from an unwanted pregnancy. The press was astounded. Well, how delighted Cardinal Winning was to be able to say, just a year later, that at least one hundred lives had been saved as a result of that initiative.

I think anyone who can give such a "testimony to the power of hope over despair" has had a great influence on the culture, and I feel sure that his gratitude for those lives will be one of the chief causes for celebration over his fifty years as a priest.

Your Eminence, may these be the words you hear when you meet Our Blessed Lord: "Well done, good and faithful servant . . . Come and join in your master's happiness"

Cardinal Paul Poupard
Pontifical Council for Culture, Vatican City

We share your sorrow and pray for his blessed soul, so dear to us at his titular Church in Rome and also to his diocese.

Padre Morosini, Superior General, Padri Minimi
Parish of Sant'Andrea delle Fratte, Rome, Italy

On each occasion we have met, Your Eminence has manifested a spiritual youthfulness. A sense of wonder and awe seems second nature to you. St Therese of Lisieux understood that holiness is nothing more or less than making one's own Jesus' teaching on spiritual childhood.

Through your priestly ministry others have seen the true nobility of their own lives. You have given witness that they are children of God.

Cardinal James Francis Stafford
President, Pontifical Council for the Laity, Vatican City

I was most especially struck by his strong dedication to Catholic education in all its forms; his support of Catholic schools has been unstinting.

Cardinal Pio Laghi
Prefect Emeritus, Congregation for Catholic Education, Vatican City

above: With Bishop Joseph Devine during a Lourdes pilgrimage.

left: Preaching at the Grotto in Lourdes.

The new Archbishop in full formal attire.

above: High jinks in a Rome hotel as the Cardinal-elect tries on his new robes.

right: The Cardinal admires his new red socks made with "Filo Scozzese" . . . Scottish thread!

The new Cardinal with the Pope.

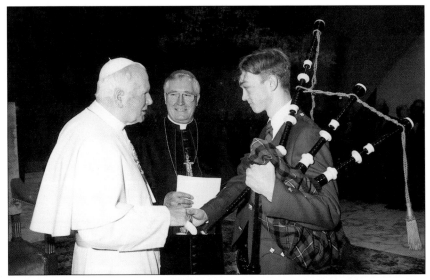

Introducing piper Iain McPhee to the Pope.

right: Receiving the red hat from John Paul II.
copyright Osservatore Romano.

below: Receiving the Cardinal's ring from John Paul II.
copyright Osservatore Romano.

Meeting the Pope after Mass with the new Cardinals.   copyright Osservatore Romano

Mass to take possession of the Cardinal's titular church in Rome, Sant'Andrea delle Fratte.

With a group of pilgrims to the Holy Land.

With the Pope, Ad Limina *visit of Scottish Bishops to Rome, 25 April 1997.*   *copyright Osservatore Romano*

Exchanging a joke during the visit with the Pope and other Scottish Bishops.   *copyright Osservatore Romano*

A meeting of European Bishops. Left of Cardinal Winning is Miloslav Vlk, a Czech priest forced to work as a window cleaner by the Communists, now a Cardinal.

Greeting Cardinal Carlo Maria Martini of Milan.

Enjoying the humour of Bishop Emeritus of Paisley, Stephen McGill.

Greeting his old friend Bishop John Jukes.

The Bishops' Conference of Scotland shortly before the Cardinal's death.

Mass at City Halls to celebrate Cardinal Winning's 50th anniversary as a priest.

A formal portrait in the Cardinal's office.

above: With Bishop Vincent Logan and the Pope during a Holy Year pilgrimage, February 2000.

left: The ordination of Fr Joe Lappin, January 7 2001. The last ordination at which the Cardinal presided.

The smiling face of the Church . . . enjoying a humorous moment during a school visit.

above: The tourist Cardinal . . . taking a photo of St Pius X's tomb in St Peter's Basilica, Rome.

left: With newly created Cardinals Murphy O'Connor (left) and Desmond Connell (right).
copyright Christopher Ginns

Cardinal Winning in Rome, February 2001.

I have had many occasions to see Cardinal Winning's sharp intellect and characteristic Scottish wit applied to important questions affecting the Universal Church, to everyone's benefit.

Cardinal Angelo Sodano
Secretary of State, Vatican City

The active pastoral concern of Cardinal Winning for the advancement of the Gospel of Life has been evidenced by such initiatives as his commitment to come to the aid of mothers who may be tempted to abort their children, and to extend to them the concrete assistance of the Church so that they may have the courage to choose life.

Cardinal Alfonso Lopez-Trujillo
Pontifical Council for the Family, Vatican City

I remember the Cardinal from his visit to Moscow a few years ago. When I suggested that he should celebrate Mass in my chapel, he said he preferred to celebrate in his room at the Russia hotel where he could look over the Kremlin and Red Square. He said he felt that he was offering Mass for Russia on Red Square itself. He had prayed so many times for the conversion of Russia from his childhood.

Archbishop Thaddaeus Kondrusiewicz
Archbishop of Moscow
President of the Russian Conference of Bishops

This is for me and many others, I am sure, more than the death of a brother archbishop and cardinal, the loss of a true and trusted friend, who will be dearly remembered.

Cardinal Jean-Marie Lustiger
Archbishop of Paris, France

I have watched with pride the role of courageous and prophetic leadership which he sustained in Scotland over the years.

Amidst all the publicity which he received, he remained his simple and unspoiled and unassuming self, always the "man of the people" always with a witty remark of joke to enliven even serious discussions.

He will be remembered as one of the great Catholic churchmen of the century, and, indeed, one of the great Scotsmen of his time. May he rest in God's eternal peace.

Cardinal Cahal B Daly
Archbishop emeritus of Armagh, Ireland

He was a true friend, one on whom I was able to rely with confidence.

Archbishop Joseph A Fiorenza
Bishop of Galveston-Houston
President, National Conference of Catholic Bishops, USA

I heard that Cardinal Thomas Winning returned to the Father. I knew him as a faithful servant of the Church and as a man with a great vision. The Lord will grant him the eternal peace and joy.

Cardinal Godfried Danneels
Archbishop of Malines-Brussels, Belgium

He was a man of deep faith and strong convictions. His Eminence had a great love for the Church and was a firm defender of her teachings.

Cardinal Anthony Bevilacqua
Archbishop of Philadelphia, USA

I remember his sweetness and friendliness, his burning pastoral zeal, profound faith and humanity, love for the poor, heartfelt support for ecumenical dialogue and intelligent and enlightening work for the European Bishops' Conferences.

Cardinal Carlo Maria Martini
Archbishop of Milan, Italy

Cardinal Winning will be remembered as a great pastor in so many fields of the apostolate, not least in the area of media. With his founding of the Archdiocesan newspaper "Flourish" and an Office for Communications, he showed his understanding of the importance of social communications in the mission of the Church. Through his own very effective presence in the mass media - not only in Scotland but in the rest of Britain – he was able to set forth clearly the Church's teaching and practice in important areas of doctrine, morality and social concern. He will be greatly missed.

Archbishop John P Foley
Pontifical Council for Social Communications, Vatican City

I count myself fortunate to have gotten to know Cardinal Winning . . . Your Archbishop, as you know so much better than I, was a man not only characterised by courage and pastoral zeal but also blessed with a wonderful vision of ecclesial collaboration and good sense of humour. His leadership and generosity in the College of Bishops will be much missed.

May the Lord raise up many other men and women in the Church today who are as determined as Cardinal Winning to proclaim the Good News, whether in season or out.

Bishop Gerald Wiesner, OMI
Bishop of Prince George, President, Canadian Conference of Catholic Bishops

Cardinal Winning was always a most engaging Church leader. It was always a special joy to be with him.

Cardinal Roger M Mahony
Archbishop of Los Angeles, USA

Carrying the Cross on the Via Dolorosa in Jerusalem.

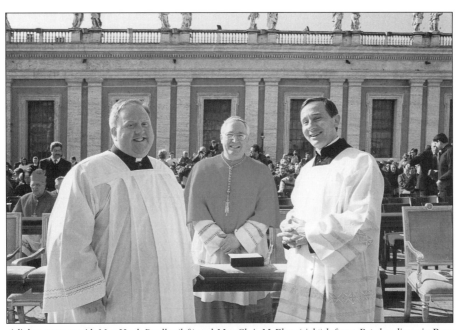

A lighter moment with Mgr Hugh Bradley (left) and Mgr Chris McElroy (right) before a Papal audience in Rome.

Enjoying a joke with some Religious Sisters in Glasgow.

Visiting an enclosed order of Carmelite nuns in Rovigo, Italy.

Our consolation at the time of death comes from the words of Our Blessed Lord, Who has promised eternal life to those who walk in His way and live by His truth during the time of their earthly pilgrimage. How faithfully Cardinal Winning lived up to this promise.

Cardinal Bernard Law
Archbishop of Boston, USA

His encouragement meant a great deal to all the people of Scotland as they acquired their own Parliament and a stronger identity in the family of nations. God rest his generous soul!

Cardinal William H Keeler
Archbishop of Baltimore, USA

He was a man of dialogue, able to play down any difficult situations; a truly European and ecumenical man; he always gave a joyful and youthful witness; he was a cardinal with a simple heart and profound humanity. Many young people were touched by this pastoral, open, serene, joyful figure, so capable of entering into dialogue.

Bishop Amedeus Grab
Bishop of Chur, Switzerland, President of Council of European Bishops' Conferences

Cardinal Thomas was a man of extraordinary vibrancy, who made it a particular point to stand close to his people. We all admired his tremendous courage in taking sides on many important issues both for the Church and for society in Scotland.

Father Timothy Radcliffe OP
Master of the Dominican Order, Rome, Italy

He was a courageous person and never hesitated to stand on the right side of the truth. I hope one would be right to say that where the angels dare to tread the Cardinal trod without fear.
We here in Nigeria identify with all of you at this period when you mourn the departure of this true Scot.

Rev Andrew Danjuma
Nigeria

I feel the loss of Tom Winning almost as if I had been one of his people. He was one I felt I could count on as a friend, for he was a priest of the people and was all-inclusive in those he debated with, laughed with and shared the Christian faith with. The whole Church in Scotland has lost a powerful voice and a good friend.

Rev. Douglas Aitken
Fife

top: Preaching at an ecumenical meeting in Glasgow SECC.

middle: Meeting Cardinals Daly (left) and Hume (right) at Glasgow's City Chambers.

bottom: Getting the message across during an ecumenical service.

Lighting the Easter Fire, a symbol of Christ bringing new light into the darkness, at the Easter Vigil ceremonies in a Glasgow parish, assisted by Diocesan Chancellor and MC, Mgr Peter Smith.

His passion for the poor as well as his firm views on such issues as abortion and sexual ethics thrust him into the public realm. There, he showed a consistency that was apparent to all. Such views may not have been universally popular but he was undaunted in communicating his own thoughts and the teachings of his Church. In these things he was not only speaking for the Roman Catholic Church but spoke for many in other denominations in Scotland and beyond.

Rev Archibald M Ford
Moderator of General Assembly
United Free Church of Scotland

He was a man who truly exemplified Christianity. He had the courage to be true to his faith in Jesus Christ and his teachings. He was outspoken in his stance against the evils of our times yet showed tender love and compassion for the poorest and underprivileged sections of our society.

Stephen C Kerr
President, Edinburgh Stake (Presbytery) of The Church of Jesus Christ of Latter-day Saints

We will remember Tom as the first Roman Catholic bishop to address the General Assembly of the Church of Scotland, a historic occasion, which enabled our two churches to put aside our bitter history and enter what was to become an increasingly positive and co-operative relationship.

Rt Rev John D Miller
Moderator of the General Assembly of the Church of Scotland

The Baptist community is grateful to God for the fearless stand he took to defend and uphold the biblical standards of morality within our national life. But we are also grateful for his compassion and the generosity of spirit with which he reached out to all, especially to those who are most vulnerable in our society.

William G Slack
General Secretary, The Baptist Union of Scotland

We Muslims were inspired frequently by the strong moral stand taken by the Cardinal on many issues, especially Pro-Life opposition to abortion and keeping section twenty-eight. What we loved most about your great Cardinal is his sincere way of speaking up with no compromise and putting clearly to the public at large the divine moral code of our God Almighty.

We all hope and pray that our religious leaders, Muslims and Christians, will follow the steps of this great Christian.

Dr A Majid Katme
Islamic Concern

Two moments during a Mass at a Glasgow parish, just months before the Cardinal's death.

Preaching at the Episcopal Ordination of Ian Murray, Bishop of Argyll and the Isles.

The laying on of hands.

Meeting Sir Leon Brittan in Brussels.

Meeting Alex Salmond and his wife Moira in Glasgow.

FAREWELL

MAN OF THE PEOPLE

There is absolutely no question in our minds that this world has lost a truly great man, a man of great courage and conviction.

We are sure that the Angels in Heaven, together with the countless thousands of little children he tried to save, will have given him a tremendous welcome to his heavenly home.

John Henry
Society for the Protection of Unborn Children, Dewsbury, England

Although obviously a person of great authority in the Church, he shed all trappings of position and became a friend to all our helpers and children. In Lourdes with HCPT, Cardinal Tom met pilgrims on a very personal level. During the last pilgrimage he accompanied us on, I met him sitting on the pavement entertaining a youngster who was afraid to go into Le Cachot because it was too busy. I'm not too sure if the child really appreciated who the helper was who was singing to him, but he was certainly enjoying the attention. Cardinal Tom was loved by the kids.

John Kerr
Handicapped Children's Pilgrimage Trust, Glasgow

There was a time when Catholic schools were under considerable pressure simply to be the same as other schools and not to emphasise their differences. There is now a self-confidence in the Catholic school system which has placed it at centre-stage on the Scottish educational scene. Much of this is due to Cardinal Winning.

We have lost a courageous and inspiring leader. No one in the history of Catholic education has made a greater contribution. He has shown us the way.

John Oates
Catholic Education Commission

All he ever wanted to be . . . a parish priest.

Man of the people . . . with a hearty appetite for song and for food!

I remember with great fondness His Eminence coming to visit the school at our prizegiving and on the occasion of the sixteen hundreth anniversary of St Ninian's arrival in Scotland. We were particularly proud that he presented us with the letter from His Holiness the Pope commemorating the anniversary of St Ninian and it is something we will always treasure.

He valued Catholic schools so much and I recall his endeavours in the 1970s to have full time Chaplains appointed to all schools in the Glasgow Archdiocese. At this time the words from *Flower of Scotland* come to my mind, "When will we see his likes again?"

Anthony Conroy
Head Teacher, St. Ninian's High School, Kirkintilloch

Tom will be sadly missed by the many School Board members who benefited from his advice and leadership. The President and Executive Board members of SSBA are honoured to have known and worked with him.

Ann Hill
Chief Executive, Scottish School Boards Association

Was it his own wish that he might be remembered as having had time for people? It was undoubtedly the case – and true in the deepest sense. He was a magnificent advert for the real meaning of the Church.

Rev Colin M Anderson
Old High Church of Inverness

We especially remember the Cardinal's commitment to the poor and the outcast, expressed with conviction publicly and lived out privately, as well as his clear stance on what he felt was the teaching of the Church on moral issues.

Alex Hughes
Commissioner, The Salvation Army, Glasgow

In many ways conservative he also had a passionate social conscience. This combination often appears in Scottish Catholicism in ways it does not in the Christian church elsewhere.

Bruce Embleton
Church Treasurer, Camrose Baptist Church

I had the honour to know Cardinal Winning over a period of many years and experienced his warmth and friendship to me and to the Jewish Community in general at first hand. My wife and I had the great pleasure of accompanying him to Rome in 1996 on the occasion of the Jubilee of his ordination as a Bishop. On that occasion he saw to it that we were looked after and guided round Rome, and we were indeed looked after to perfection. We were hardly his top priority, but he made us feel as though we were.

Henry Tankel
Jewish Community, Glasgow

During a visit to Africa.

Enjoying a meal with members of Glasgow's Sikh community.

With the late Jock Stein at a reception in Glasgow's City Chambers.

Telling it as it is at a pro-life rally in Glasgow.

*Meeting the youth
of Latin America
during a visit to
the shanty towns
of Brazil.*

A solemn moment during a Papal Ceremony in St Peter's Square.

With First Minister Henry McLeish and the then-Scottish Secretary John Reid at a Papal Audience to mark the 400th anniversary of the Scots College in Rome, December 2000.

copyright Osservatore Romano

"Give me back my hat!" . . . *a moment of fun in the Gorbals.*

In fancy dress during a visit to Africa.

At an honorary degree ceremony.

Relaxing with long-time friend Mgr Pedro Lopez-Gallo in Vancouver.

Provoking merriment during a conference in Cambridge in July 2000.   copyright Lorenzo Lees.

With Scottish civic leaders in Rome, December 2000.

Pressing the flesh . . . greetings from a young fan.

Meeting Irish President Mary McAleese.

With former Celtic supremo Fergus McCann and former Moderator of the General Assembly of the Church of Scotland, Very Rev Sandy McDonald at the launch of a campaign against bigotry.

With the then-Scottish Education Minister Sam Galbraith at the opening of St Mary's School, Bishopbriggs.

School visits . . . informal. above, and formal, below.

If the cap fits, wear it! With children of Corpus Christi Primary School.   copyright Hugh Dougherty

Meeting a young admirer after a Lourdes Day celebration in Easterhouse.

Enjoying a laugh with Lourdes pilgrims.

Looking back on newspaper cuttings at a civic reception.

School Assembly with a Prince of the Church at St Matthew's Primary, Bishopbriggs.

Risking life and limb with the children.

A thoughtful moment under the gaze of the TV cameras.

copyright Celtic View.

Last visit to Celtic Park, May 2001.

A man of love and compassion who will always reign in the hearts of the Scottish people. I too have good reason to remember Cardinal Winning with love. I will always pray for his soul and remember that all his good deeds go with him.

Marie Edwards

"A Glasgow granny living in Australia."

I was going to go and see him in hospital, but I knew he'd have a lot of visitors and thought I'd wait until he got home. I wish I had gone now. He was a great guy and a real carer. He was a man loved by the people, including people who weren't Catholics.

I oversaw the auction of the Cardinal's famous *red hat* which raised £7,000. Afterward he said "next year I'll get you the Pope's one" and I thought he was kidding. But next year he showed up with one of the Pope's white hats – it went for £26,000, it was incredible. I am really saddened, I am going to miss him.

Andy Cameron

Comedian

My brother Jimmy and myself were on our way to Derry, on the Sea Cat heading for Belfast. Being the sophisticates we are, we were sitting having a burger and fries (large!) when I spotted the Cardinal. Being neither shy nor retiring, I greeted him and he immediately came over and joined us. He was on his way to something important; we were on our way to present the prizes at a dinner dance for the pigeon fanciers of Derry!

We spoke of matters of great consequence, 'doos' and the Hoops! That he was familiar with some of the subtle nuances of 'doo' racing, highlighted the fact that he had not forgotten his very ordinary origins.

Although he was with members of his family, the Cardinal had time for us.

Fr Eddie McGhee

Galloway

Although inundated with inquiries when he became cardinal, Tom took time to answer The Diary's questions. When we asked what the new job meant, he said: "The word cardinal derives from the Latin for hinge. Someone told me a hinge works best when it is well-oiled, but I don't think that applies to Cardinals!"

Tom Shields and Ken Smith

Herald Diary

The Church has certainly lost a great man. In recent years his stand on Pro-Life issues and other moral issues was a tremendous help for us all. He really was getting the message of the Church across through the media.

I only met the Cardinal once when I visited him in March 2000 to introduce myself and keep him informed about our apostolic work in Glasgow. It is harder to imagine a more friendly and entertaining man.

Rev Mgr Nicholas Morrish

Regional Vicar, Opus Dei, London

Humour was a characteristic the Cardinal cherished. The young student who translated the Celtic football team into Latin and slipped them into the Litany of the Saints, the auxiliary bishop who would whip off his purple skull cap and turn it inside out revealing the white lining, and quip: "In case of a quick promotion." He even pondered choosing *Christus Vincit* as his Latin motto so schoolboys would translate it as "Christ is Winning!"

Stephen McGinty
The Scotsman, 18 June 2001

His birth into eternal life leaves you feeling sad and bereft. We also loved him and held him in the utmost regard for his candour and his apostolic courage as well as his warmth of humanity.

Fr Feargal P. McGrady CC
Parish of Drumbo and Carryduff, Belfast

Although I never had the opportunity to meet you I somehow feel that I knew you and I think this world is going to be a much lesser place without you. I suppose it's a golden opportunity for the rest of us to pick up where you left off. God bless and hopefully one day we will get to meet and no doubt we'll discuss the Bhoys too.

Mick Gavin
via e-mail

The Cardinal was a neighbour for almost ten years in Newlands and we were both Lanarkshire people too. I knew him early on in his priesthood and he never lost sight of his background and upbringing. He was always happy in the company of the Lisbon Lions and came along to help launch our website and was on great form. We'll remember him fondly as a humble and straightforward person.

Billy McNeill
Former Captain and Manager of Celtic FC

What a wonderful courageous Cardinal. His voice was known not only on the European front of the Church, but here in North America and very much in Canada. I followed many of his stances on so many issues especially that on behalf of the unborn children.

From his place in Heaven he will surely work even harder for the Church and for Her faithful on earth and I believe he will always "do a little extra for us Catholic Scots".

Maria Dalgarno
Canada

Always a hit with the children . . . two moments from school visits in the early 1970s.

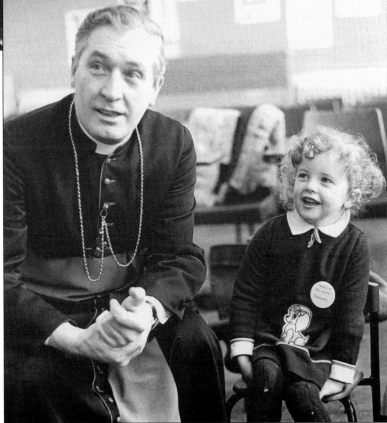

Formal or informal . . . a man at home with all age groups.

His public persona was often that of a hard, uncompromising man, but those who worked with him and shared time with him, knew that in reality he was a very warm human being.

I had the privilege to be with the Cardinal as he led the celebrations to mark the four-hundreth anniversary of the Scots College in Rome. How he loved that. He had studied for the priesthood in Rome and the college and the city held a very special place in his heart. He was well known in his favourite restaurants there and was always greeted as a friend, welcome and at home among them.

He loved people and enjoyed nothing more than spending time with them. Prince of the Church he may have been, but he was down-to-earth, singularly lacking in any airs and graces.

On the pilgrimages, everybody wanted a piece of him, everybody wanted to talk to him. And he made time for them all. Each night at dinner, he sat not with his beloved sister Margaret or his loyal housekeeper Mrs Mac, but wherever there was a seat. No one person was more important than any other to him. Everybody mattered.

His energy and stamina for a man of his age was remarkable, and as we walked round all the holy places he was always watching out for those not quite as able as they once were, many it has to be said, who were younger than the man himself!

On another occasion, during a pilgrimage to the Holy Land, at the Wailing Wall, all men have to wear skull caps in accordance with Jewish tradition. They are picked at random out of a bag as the pilgrims make their way to the holy site. The Cardinal just happened to pick a white one. Papal? I asked him, "Naw, just paper, that'll do me," he replied.

Elaine Harrison
Journalist

I will always treasure the memory of a meal in Cambridge when I was at table at dinner with the Cardinal and Bishop Conti. The wonderful banter and good natured joshing reminded me of a father teasing his grown-up children over the dinner table. I think it is somehow appropriate that he went to the Lord on Father's Day because he was a real father to us all.

Paul Burnell
Journalist

He was a romantic idealist whose hopes were not idle dreams but expressions of a commitment to Christian values and a conviction that in God's good time and through our endeavours the values of the Kingdom might be more extensively embraced. In the central Scotland of his childhood a Catholic might easily expect to be discriminated against, socially excluded and even physically assaulted.

Notwithstanding the sectarian bigotry highlighted in James Macmillan's account of *Scotland's Shame*, the fact of the matter is that Catholics now take their place in society, and some – such as Thomas Winning – even manage to be leaders of it.

He preached in season and out, and challenged new orthodoxies as well as old heresies. Scotland is a better country for his life and work and is a poorer one for his passing.

Professor John Haldane
Department of Philosophy, University of St Andrews

I knew him for almost thirty years and he was always very kind to me. I truly feel that I have lost a friend. He was a great man who will be genuinely missed by everyone.

David Marshall MP
Shettleston, Glasgow

He was a unique combination of three great qualities – courage, compassion and conviction. His spirited leadership was a tremendous inspiration to our family and the wider Christian community.

Brian Souter
Perth

He was a very great man, and I had a long and happy relationship with him both as a Scottish Minister for Education and as an MSP.

One of the highlights of my life was to be his guest at a lunch, when I received wonderful pasta which he had cooked.

Lord James Douglas Hamilton MSP
Edinburgh

Knowing of his great concern for the poor of the world from our meetings on international development as well as recalling his commitments, his modesty and humour on various occasions – outside Celtic Park; at Donald Dewar's funeral; on the *Daily Record* march against drugs and many other occasions – I realise how widely he will be missed.

The sense of loss is as great among those of us who do not share the Catholic faith as it undoubtedly is in the Catholic community.

George Foulkes MP, Minister of State
Scotland Office, London

Meeting the new bishop . . . these children look as pleased as punch!

With young relatives at a civic reception.

Without the late Cardinal's contribution then our modern Scotland would be much less of a nation.

Thomas Winning's great ambition was to have the Catholic Church fully accepted as part of the infrastructure of Scottish society. In this he has succeeded.

Alex Salmond MP
House of Commons, London

Just occasionally in life you meet a man who not only knows what he believes but is unashamed and unabashed about telling you. Cardinal Thomas Winning is one of these rare men – and you don't have to be a Scot to thank God for him.

If he had not spoken out during the 1997 General Election, issues such as abortion would never have been raised. His life-saving initiatives in offering vulnerable women an alternative to abortion eloquently demonstrate how words need to be backed up by action. We don't just owe him our thanks – there are some who owe him their lives.

Lord (David) Alton
House of Lords, London

The Catholic Church could not have asked for a more stout defender of its cause than Thomas Winning. In every sense, he was a very intelligent, articulate disciple of Rome and he will be a great loss to the Church and also to the wider Scottish community.

Rt Hon Eric Milligan
Lord Provost, Edinburgh

He was immensely accessible, full of humanity and humour, and the unborn child could not have wished for a finer champion.

Countess Josephine Quintavalle
Pro-Life Alliance, London

Everyone has noted his very special love for the poor and marginalised. Those of us who work with children who have special needs have first-hand experience of his compassion and pastoral care for our young people and their families. He will indeed be greatly missed but, as well as being so much a man of the people, he was also such a prayerful man of God that we trust he is now enjoying the fullness of His Presence.

Sr Patricia Gribbin, SND
Head Teacher, Kelvin School, Glasgow

The good things he did were legion. He elevated Scotland's Catholics from their position as a rather despised sect into part of the mainstream community; he fearlessly condemned abortion and backed up his rhetoric with practical measures; he spoke up not just for Catholics but for huge numbers of people in debates about morality. In short, perhaps Tom Winning's greatest contribution to Scottish life was that he was a noisy Cardinal at a time when noise was required.

Katie Grant

Journalist

He was without doubt a great, strong leader, a great priest and a great Scot.

Sir Tom Farmer

Businessman

He was the most controversial British prelate of recent times, a bull in the ecclesiastical china shop. He was reviled by much of the establishment, and returned its contempt with interest. Cardinal Winning was too socialist for New Labour, too conservative for the Conservatives, too internationalist for the Nationalists and too Christian for any of them

He was a great churchman who spent his life trying to build the City of God on the streets of Glasgow

Daily Telegraph

Editorial, 18 June 2001

above: Humour knows no age barriers!

left: In case of quick promotion!

Off duty, enjoying the sights in Venice.

"Who said I can't sing?"

"So you want to be a footballer when you grow up do you?"

Presenting the prizes at the Cardinal's Ball.

Signing autographs.

An interview in Rome for STV's Eikon programme.

In front of the cameras again, this time in support of SCIAF.

Upstaging old friend Andy Cameron at the Cardinal's Ball.

FAREWELL

FRIEND

Fidelis ad Deum et Caledonia ad finem. (Faithful to God and to Scotland, to the end.)

M. Robertson
via e-mail

He will be able to take pride (through Christ's treasury of merits and abundant grace) at Our Lord's mandate: "Whatsoever you did for the least of my brothers you did for me." Tom, you put most of us to shame. *Oremus pro invicem.* (Let us pray for one another.)

John
via e-mail

You were a far better man than you thought you were, and a far better shepherd than we thought you were. You are sorely missed.

Jack
via e-mail

Thomas you were the defender of the weak and helpless and you spoke for those who had no words. May these angelic infants come to greet you as you enter into the joy of your Lord. With prayers and love from an Anglican sister.

Sister Clare Lockhart
via e-mail

My heart goes out to the beloved land of Scotland which mourns the shepherd it has lost. His life was spent labouring for ordinary people, for the defenceless, for children and for the Church. My first thoughts are of those unforgettable days of a year and a half ago when he came to Rovigo and delivered a determined and passionate speech to the convention organised by the Italian Pro-Life Movement. Still I recall so many memorable phrases from his address.

He said that we could never hope to change the law if first we did not change people's hearts. He spoke of the responsibility of each of us in the office, in the classroom, in the surgery and in the factory to be an apostle of life. And he spoke of abortion and euthanasia as crimes which had been turned into rights.

But his most memorable advice to us was when he said that too often arguments against the culture of death are not accompanied by acts of friendship, of love and of compassion. His own Pro-life Initiative, which we admired so much, was an example of love and compassion being shown to those faced with the temptation to abort.

Dr Luca Busson
Italian Pro-Life Movement, Rovigo, Italy

Signing the condolence book.

Prince Edward arrives for the funeral, accompanied by Mgr Noel Woods
copyright Kieran Chambers

To a friend I never knew, but knew I always had. Love and prayers. xx

Anonymous

A happy man who loved everybody

Sarah Killin
(From Book of Condolences, Glasgow City Chambers)

You made them think!

Gary McKay,
(From Book of Condolences, Glasgow City Chambers)

You lived your life according to your beliefs – You did not deviate from what you believed to be right – and you were the greatest follower of the catechism I have ever known!

Margaret McCafferty
(From Book of Condolences, Glasgow City Chambers)

I met you more than once. Hope to meet you again in a better place

Margaret Keenan
(From Book of Condolences, Glasgow City Chambers)

Life is a journey we travel and God watches over us. To the man who changed and made my life . . . may you rest in God's hands.

Hugh McEwan
(From Book of Condolences, West Dunbartonshire Council)

Poor St Peter, the Cardinal will never give him a moment's rest!

John Kane
(From Book of Condolences, West Dunbartonshire Council)

Thank you for making us feel we mattered and belonged

Patricia Walker
(From Book of Condolences, West Dunbartonshire Council)

Thank you for being our Cardinal

Elizabeth Clarke
(From Book of Condolences, St John the Baptist, Port Glasgow)

You will never walk alone!

S McGhee
(From Book of Condolences, St John the Baptist, Port Glasgow)

Thank you Thomas, you gave your life to us.

John Higgins
(From Book of Condolences, St John the Baptist, Port Glasgow)

His love of his family was an inspiration to very many. And I remember on my visits with him to Rome the regular journeys to Piazza Navona to see the cribs when we were there in Advent, with the Cardinal carefully considering what other figures he should bring home! Further, we also journeyed to the toy shops in Borgo Pio, again to see what treasures and delights were to be brought home to his great nephews and great nieces – always being carefully tried out by the Cardinal beforehand with deep chuckles of laughter.

Archbishop Keith Patrick O'Brien
Archbishop of St Andrew's and Edinburgh

I have lost not only a brother bishop but a good friend.

I well remember those minutes seventeen years ago when he phoned me on a Wednesday morning and asked me to come and see him. I asked him if I could come on Thursday instead as Wednesday was my day off!

However I went on Wednesday and with his sense of fun bursting through he said: "John, how would you like to be a bishop?"

I really thought he was teasing me in his usual impish way. It took me some time to realise he was serious and that Rome was waiting for a reply. I felt so honoured to be invited to work for the salvation of souls, with one I admired so much.

He aimed to bring the Church into the modern world and make its message relevant to people's lives. He was guided by the opening words of the document *Gaudium et Spes*: "The joy, the hope, the grief and anguish of the people of our time, especially of those who are poor or afflicted, are the joy and hope, the grief and anguish of the followers of Christ as well." He worked himself to death putting those words into practice.

Bishop John Mone
Bishop of Paisley

Reared in the new heartland of Scottish Catholicism and educated in the heart of Roman Catholicism he bore the hallmark of the typical Scottish Catholic of his time – proud to be Scots: proud to be "Roman". That is a tradition with a long pedigree.

We mourn his passing while celebrating his life and his achievements. May God grant him eternal rest and the reward of his good works.

Bishop Ian Murray
Bishop of Argyll and the Isles

Cardinal Winning's old friend, Cardinal Cormac Murphy O'Connor speaks at the Funeral Mass.

The clergy precede the Cardinal's coffin to its final resting place.

His sudden death has brought grief to so many. Not only because he had become so important a figure for the Church and nationally, but also because it is hard to connect such a lively, vivacious, still youthful personality with death.

Someone asked me if I thought the Cardinal tried deliberately to be controversial. I am sure that he didn't, but neither did he mind being controversial if the issue demanded it.

He lacked all pomposity, never put on airs and graces, and without warning could say something quite mischievous or make a remark both irreverent and irrelevant. No wonder I have heard people say, with amusement or even with pride, "He's an awful man".

Thank God for the gifts and opportunities which he gave to Tom Winning to be such a power for good. But we must also be grateful to the Cardinal that he used his talents – fearlessly, courageously, with a simplicity and directness that was sometimes breathtaking and always effective.

Bishop Maurice Taylor
Bishop of Galloway

Personally, I am shattered and deeply, deeply saddened by the death of Cardinal Tom.

The Catholic community in Scotland has lost a great leader, and I, along with my brother bishops, have lost a very good friend and colleague.

It has been a privilege to work with him for the last twenty years – years in which he was constant source of wisdom and support. He was a man of great strength and vigour, of humour, of unswerving loyalty, dedicated to the service of others. Above all he was a man of great faith who resolutely proclaimed the Good News of the Gospel and the Church's teaching and never wavered from that, even in the face of fierce personal attacks.

His death is a huge loss to all of us who worked in close collaboration with him and who were his friends.

Life will not be the same without him.

Bishop Vincent Logan,
Bishop of Dunkeld

There is a Latin saying: *De mortuis nihil nisi bonum*, which means that of those who have died you should say nothing but what is good. This has not been difficult in Cardinal Winning's case, as the evidence of the press and the other media of communication has shown.

As a leader he was outstanding and outspoken; outstanding because he was prepared to lead; outspoken because he confronted directly the issues of the day. Time and time again his words were widely welcomed even if politically unpopular.

Already much has been said about his social radicalism – but it was the radicalism of the Gospel. He was of a piece – not a contradiction in political and spiritual matters. His whole life was orientated to Christ and sustained by a deep and devout faith.

He was "The People's Cardinal" to whom we will all be indebted for many years to come.

Bishop Mario Conti
Bishop of Aberdeen

I have many, many personal memories flooding back to me of his first retreat when he came to Blairs during the war; of his splendid work as Minute Secretary when I was Secretary to the Hierarchy – he readily accepted suggestions and vastly improved the presentation of the minutes; when he was nominated Auxiliary to Glasgow I gave him his first pectoral cross, zucchetto and purple socks – the pre-Vatican purple socks he thought a great joke.

When I came to celebrate my fortieth anniversary of episcopal consecration it was Cardinal Tom who preached the homily – he did me proud and gave a splendid expose of the Priesthood. Strangely though the other Bishops called me Steve he could never bring himself to be so familiar!

Bishop Stephen McGill
Bishop Emeritus of Paisley

An era has ended; the mould has been broken. A great leader has been taken from us and none of us has as yet come to terms with the shock and the enormity of our loss. In addition to being our spiritual leader the Cardinal was the voice of conscience; not just the Catholic conscience but the conscience surely of every God-fearing Scot of whatever denomination. And no one else had ever filled that role.

The Preface of the Requiem Mass contains that seminal sentence: "Lord for your faithful people life is changed, not ended". With the death of our beloved Cardinal, life is changed. Not just for the Catholic Church in Scotland and abroad, but for all of us whose lives had been touched by this fearless yet lovely man. Every single one of us who had the privilege of knowing him is the better and the richer for the experience.

Len Murray
Friend and Glasgow Lawyer

If he could speak to us yet, I think I knew him well enough to convey that final message. It would be this. "Don't waste your tears on me, though I am grateful for them. Instead, say your prayers for me. I will be even more grateful for them."

A right of reply? Certainly the Cardinal would give us that, as our final farewell to him. If I am any judge, I am going to presume that you will let me voice for you what you would want me to say. It is not more than six simple words. The words are these: "Tom, thank you for being you."

Bishop Joseph Devine
Bishop of Motherwell

The priests (above) and the people (below) of Glasgow bid their fond farewell.

Outside (above) and inside (below) the atmosphere was one of prayerful recollection.

Cardinal Murphy O'Connor incenses the coffin of Cardinal Winning.

EPILOGUE:

LAST TUESDAY EVENING, shortly before I left home for yet another Confirmation, Mgr Peter Smith, the Chancellor here, phoned me with an offer that I could scarcely refuse. I said to him, "Peter, I have been dreading this moment for years". That moment is this moment, when I try to capture something of the life of the man who was a superstar of the Catholic Church in Scotland in the twentieth century.

It is a near impossible task, for how do you capture the "will o' the wisp" in anything? But my starting point is obvious, to convey the condolences of all who have come from beyond the Archdiocese to the Cardinal's sister Margaret, her children Agnes and Edward and their families, his devoted housekeeper for 30 years, Mrs Isabel McInnes, as well as to the priests and people of Glasgow.

Thomas Joseph Winning was a priest for over 50 years, a bishop for 30 years and a Cardinal for the past 7 years. He packed at least the content of 4 lives into his 76 years of life, due to his boundless energy and his sheer zest for life.

Since his ordination in Rome in 1948, the Church asked him to undertake virtually every office in the book, as an assistant priest, as the diocesan secretary, as spiritual director in our Roman college, as a parish priest, as the secretary of the Bishops' Conference and as Officialis of the National Tribunal, as well as the more demanding roles that he was asked to meet over the past 30 years.

His response to each and all was ready and affirmative. But that was him, ever the Church's man from his earliest days in his beloved home parish of St. Patrick's in Shieldmuir.

There was only ever one ambition in the life of Thomas Winning, to serve God in the priesthood of the Catholic Church. He was pure gold in that vocation and the Church recognised that time and time again. His work rate was legendary, as was his warmth and affection for all manner of people. At most of the functions that he attended, he was virtually the last to leave, going out "with the sawdust", to use an old Glasgow expression. All of that must have taken its toll on him, even if this was to go unnoticed until the last few days of his life.

Nor did he take time off for leisure pursuits. When he did, it would be for reading, for he was a voracious reader of the press and the best theological journals, ever interested in being up to date with all the issues that were shaping the Church or the trends shaping society. A second was an occasional walk by the sea and the third, rather more frequent visits to a well known football stadium in the east end of Glasgow.

Two things more than most endeared him to people. My mother, who had never met him at that time, said to me 27 years ago, "Joseph, what I like about our new Archbishop is that he is a fighter". Undoubtedly that was true. He went on to challenge Margaret Thatcher about the poll tax and the Falklands War. He challenged the present Prime Minister over the alleged gagging of Labour MPs who supported the cause of pro-life. He challenged the Scottish Executive about the repeal of Section 28. Just a month ago, he challenged this city about the attitude of some of its citizens to asylum seekers. He had a natural talent for the dust of battle.

The other thing that endeared him to people was his quick wit and sense of humour. Years ago, he told us of a phone call that he had received one evening at home, a weekday evening, one of the few weekday evenings when he was at home. It was from an anonymous Glasgow lady who phoned him and asked about the cost of a trip to Lourdes.

She had no idea that she was speaking to the Archbishop. She thought that she was speaking to his secretary. He began by saying, "Well, it all depends". Before he managed to say another word, in she came with the verdict, "You're just as bad as Coyle and Chambers for that's what they said, it all depends".

She was referring to Fr. Joe Coyle and Fr. Joe Chambers who were fellow curates at St. Alphonus, just on the other side of the Briggait from here. The Archbishop then said: "But they're right, it all depends on whether you want to go by air, or by train, or by coach".

"Oh, I see", she said, rather disconsolately. Suspecting that there was still more to come from this challenging caller, he then said to her: "So are you a parishioner in St. Alphonsus?" "No, I am not" she said, "I am a parishioner of . . ." then naming another parish quite close by. The Archbishop then said, "Why don't you go there?"

"Oh", she said, "That wee blighter down there would bore you to death". He loved that kind of thing and that kind of thing would happen to him over and over again.

To go to the other end of the spectrum, quite literally, some time later he attended a dinner hosted by the Queen at Holyrood House, for the great and good of the land. As the meal ended, the guests formed into groups and the Queen went to meet each. The ecclesiastics grouped together, the Moderator, the Episcopal Primus and the Archbishop.

After greeting each, she turned to the Archbishop and said, "You will know that we have recently been to Rome. It was wonderful to meet the Holy Father and we found so helpful the Cardinal Secretary of State. But we could never remember his name. So, privately, Philip and I used to call him Cardinal Saucepan". "Close enough, Your Majesty", he replied, "for his name is Casaroli!"

In May of 1982, with Archbishop Worlock of Liverpool, he gained much credit, for keeping on track the visit of the Holy Father to Britain which had been threatened by the war in the Falklands. They found a formula that everyone had wanted by inviting the Argentinian Cardinals of the day to come to Rome and making them aware that John Paul's visit was of a purely pastoral nature and was not in any sense a kind of quasi-state visit. This was cemented by a public display of unity on the Sunday prior to the arrival of the Pope, when students from the Venerabile College (from England), the Scots College and Argentinian students from the Pio Latino College provided the servers at a televised Mass from St. Peter's.

As the years went on, the Cardinal was to prove no less resourceful in finding solutions to many another difficult situations.

Totally unreported by the press and the media, it was around the same time that he began his most ambitious programme, that of a pastoral plan for the spiritual and pastoral renewal of the Archdiocese. This was hardly headline grabbing stuff, but it meant so much to him over the past 20 years that he would have seen it as his own lasting legacy to the Archdiocese.

He prefaced it by introducing a ministry to priests programme and the Renew programme. We tend to forget that he was very long sighted, never banking on short-term advantage but on long term success.

At the same time – and this was to increase with the passing of the years – he was superbly gifted in pressing the button that would grab a headline, ever in relation to controversial moral and social issues. The press and the media always knew that he would come up with a different comment from the run of the mill answers that would never make a headline. He was ever good copy and he knew it.

However, as the years went by, he confided to one of his close advisors, "I wonder what the papers will say about me after I am dead? I am not worried about me, but I would hate my family to be hurt because of what the press might say". For once he got it spectacularly wrong. The press reports since last Monday have been very positive, with only a few dissenting voices. I take this opportunity of thanking the press and the media for their support of the death of a very great Archbishop, the longest serving Archbishop of Glasgow since the restoration of the hierarchy in Scotland some 123 years ago.

His faults and shortcomings? Of course there were a few, but they were all so very characteristic of the man that they were almost like minor virtues. The first was his low threshold of boredom, not least when on holiday. He was always on the move, wanting to be off somewhere, do something different, try something different to eat, go shopping and have a picnic at lunchtime while planning where to go for dinner in the evening.

A second was over-quick reactions to something that had happened and overstating his response. The third was his ability to insult his closest friends, because he knew, that they knew, that he did not mean it.

What an extraordinary life he led. What was not extraordinary was his personal spirituality. Like the man himself, it was direct and uncomplicated. Not for him the exotic or the esoteric. With him it was ever as straight as a die, the celebration of the Eucharist each day, the divine office, the rosary and quiet times in his chapel. It was like breathing to him, central and pivotal to his daily living.

Nine years ago he suffered a great loss with the death of his closest friend of 45 years, Bishop Donny Renfrew. For years Donny had suffered a poor quality of life. When the end came, it came with unexpected speed. At his Requiem Mass in St. Peter's in Partick, the Cardinal preached the finest – as well as the shortest – homily that I ever heard him deliver.

He started by saying that he stared at a blank sheet of paper on the previous day, unable to find a way to start. However, as he glanced out into the garden, a blackbird began to sing. His reaction was: "I know what I will do. I will tell them about the things that made Donny sing . . ."

It was an inspirational beginning to a remarkable homily. A couple of hours later we were back here for the interment of Bishop Renfrew in the crypt below. As the big iron door closed in the crypt, the Cardinal turned and the two of us looked at each other. He gave that characteristic smile with a shrug of the shoulders. He had guessed that I knew what he had been thinking. What he was thinking was that the next time that door was to be opened, it would be for him. Sadly, this is that day.

But not then, not yet, not for a while. There were still mountains to climb, lots of them as it turned out. There was his continuing work with Bishops' Conference of which he has been President over the past 16 years. There was his work for and with the Education Commission, of which he was the president for the past 25 years. Best of all, there was the day when the Holy Father announced that the Archbishop of Glasgow was to be created Cardinal at the concistory in November 1994. Over 1500 Scots went to Rome for him and with him for that wonderful occasion. It was not an honour that he ever thought would come his way, not least as he bought a new set of a bishop's purple robes just a couple of months before the announcement.

But his membership of the Sacred College only served to increase his workload at home and abroad. Lots of parishes over the country here, not only in Glasgow, but in every diocese in Scotland wanted to see the Scottish Cardinal. Maybe his greatest fault lay in his inability to say no to such invitations. But then he was ever a people person. On his death certificate it may say that the cause of his death was a heart attack. That is true, superficially. The real truth is that Cardinal Winning died of having lived.

The last time he was in the Cathedral in Motherwell was for me, a year ago, when I celebrated a 40th anniversary of ordination. Around 800 people were there, all of whom were invited to the parish hall for some simple refreshments after Mass. He was in great form, as he was back close to home, in a parish were he had served over 40 years before. Nor was his quick wit to desert him. So crowded was the hall that neither the Cardinal nor I could make our way inside. So we stood in the foyer and greeted people as they left. Near to the end of the evening, out came Fran and Anna, the well known sister duet singing couple from Coatbridge, attired as ever in identical tartan suits with hats that sported an ostrich feather at least two feet high.

They came over to see me first and asked me to sign the Mass brochure. Then they went to take their leave of himself. For those who do not know them, they are the kind of Catholics who would kneel to kiss the Cardinal's ring. Then they left, among the last to do so. But they had not gone far when they turned back, as they had forgotten to get the Cardinal to sign their Mass brochures. By then he was speaking to someone else. Respectfully, they stood and waited until the person left. The Cardinal then turned around suddenly being again confronted with the sight of Fran and Anna. As quick as a flash he said, "I thought that there was only two of you"!

I chose the readings for today with the Cardinal very much in mind. For someone who had lost half of his stomach 40 years ago, can you imagine a banquet that will go on forever and in a setting that will be eternally home? I chose the second as I have never known anyone so well who had such an influence on others and to the times in which he lived. So huge was that impact, that he would not have believed the widespread depth of mourning at the news of his death. Thousands have passed his coffin in the past few days and many more thousands would have wished to have done so. I chose the Gospel passage as it resonates with the values of the Kingdom of God, the central values that he advocated in all seasons to a flock whom he knew well and who well knew him.

Two years to the day, he died on the same date as Cardinal Hume, 17th June. But 17th June this year was the feast of Corpus Christi, the Body of Christ. The Church is also the body of Christ. What a fitting day for him to die. He had worked for the Church and fought for the Church all his life. His motto contained one of those two words, Christi, "*Caritas Christi urget nos*", the love of Christ spurs us on. How well he lived up to the meaning of that motto.

As I draw towards a conclusion, my thoughts return to you, Margaret, to Agnes and Edward, to the children and to Mrs McInnes. You were such an important part of his life. The past week must have seemed almost interminable to you. Now it is near its end. Yet perhaps for you the hardest part is soon to come. To you he was simply Tom, or uncle Tom, or Father.

To his Eminence of Westminster and to thousands of others, he was simply Tom as well. Years ago, the old sacristan at Nazareth House in Glasgow, a former merchant seaman, met the Archbishop for the first time when he came to offer Mass for the Sisters and the residents one Christmas morning in the early 1980s. We all know what that old man meant when he greeted the Archbishop as follows, "Your Grace", he said, "what I like most about you is that you have no dignity", for Thomas Joseph Cardinal Winning never stood on his dignity, ever.

Finally, if he could speak to us yet, I think I knew him well enough to convey that final message. It would be this. Don't waste your tears on me, though I am grateful for them. Instead, say your prayers for me. I will be even more grateful for them. All of you here, along with the hundreds of people linked to us in 6 other churches in the Archdiocese and people watching this Requiem Mass on television in their own homes, assuredly, all of you have prayed for him and will continue to pray for him.

A right of reply? Certainly the Cardinal would give us that, as our final farewell to him. If I am any judge, I am going to presume that you will let me voice for you what you would want me to say. It is not more than six simple words. Those words are these – "Tom, thank you for being you".

Amen.

The symbols that sum up a life . . . a book of the Gospels, the Cardinal's red biretta, his chalice and his stole.